Mark

Genesis—Leon J. Wood
Exodus—F. B. Huey, Jr.
Leviticus—Louis Goldberg
Numbers—F. B. Huey, Jr.
Deuteronomy—Louis Goldberg
Joshua—Paul P. Enns
Judges—Paul P. Enns
Ruth—Paul P. Enns
1, 2 Samuel—Howard F. Vos
1 2 Kings—Howard F. Vos
1, 2 Chronicles—Eugene H. Merrill
Ezra, Nehemiah, Esther—Howard F. Vos
Job—D. David Garland
*Psalms— Ronald B. Allen
Proverbs—Eldon Woodcock
Ecclesiastes—Louis Goldberg
Song of Songs—Edward M. Curtis
Isaiah—D. David Garland
Jeremiah—F. B. Huey, Jr.
Lamentations—Dan G. Kent
Ezekiel—Paul P. Enns
Daniel—Leon J. Wood
Hosea—D. David Garland
Joel—Ronald B. Allen
Amos—D. David Garland
Obadiah, Jonah—John H. Walton and Bryan E. Beyer
Micah—Jack R. Riggs
Nahum, Habakkuk, Zephaniah, Haggai—J. N. Boo Heflin
Zechariah—Homer Heater, Jr.
Malachi—Charles D. Isbell
Matthew—Howard F. Vos
Mark—Howard F. Vos
Luke—Virtus E. Gideon
John—Herschel H. Hobbs
Acts—Curtis Vaughan
Romans—Curtis Vaughan and Bruce Corley
1 Corinthians—Curtis Vaughan and Thomas D. Lea
2 Corinthians—Aída B. Spencer and William D. Spencer
Galatians—Curtis Vaughan
Ephesians—Curtis Vaughan
Philippians—Howard F. Vos
Colossians and Philemon—Curtis Vaughan
The Thessalonian Epistles—John F. Walvoord
The Pastoral Epistles—E. M. Blaiklock
Hebrews—Leon Morris
James—Curtis Vaughan
1, 2 Peter, Jude—Curtis Vaughan and Thomas D. Lea
1, 2, 3 John—Curtis Vaughan
Revelation—Alan F. Johnson

*Not yet published as of this printing.

BIBLE STUDY COMMENTARY

Mark

HOWARD F. VOS

Lamplighter Books Grand Rapids, Michigan
Zondervan Publishing House

MARK: A BIBLE STUDY COMMENTARY
© 1978 by The Zondervan Corporation
Grand Rapids, Michigan

Lamplighter Books are published by Zondervan
Publishing House, 1415 Lake Drive, S.E.,
Grand Rapids, Michigan 49506

Library of Congress Cataloging in Publication Data

Vos, Howard Frederic, 1925–
    Mark: a study guide commentary.

    Bibliography: p
    1. Bible.   N.T.   Mark—Study.
BS2586.V67   226'.3'07   78-8685
ISBN 0-310-33873-5

Printed in the United States of America

90 91 92 93 94 95 / EP / 10 9 8 7 6 5

Contents

Chapter 1

Background

The Gospel of Mark appeals especially to men and women on the go. The book is full of action. Within the first twenty verses alone the writer introduces the ministry of John the Baptist, the baptism of Jesus, the temptation of Jesus, the arrest of John the Baptist, and Jesus' calling of His first four disciples. Forty-one times in the sixteen chapters Mark uses an adverb translated variously as "straightway," "forthwith," or "immediately." He frequently connects one narrative to another with the conjunction "and," as if he hardly had time for a pause. On scores of occasions he uses the historical present (e.g., "the Spirit *driveth* him into the wilderness," 1:12) or the imperfect tense, both of which picture action as in process. In keeping with this almost breathless description of the life and work of Christ, there is no genealogy and very little attention to discourse. The teachings of Christ generally rise out of His activity. For its length, this Gospel gives more attention than any of the others to the miracles of Jesus, describing eighteen of the thirty-five specifically recorded in the Gospels.

The Book of Mark also appeals to active people because of its vividness—the kind of vividness that comes from eyewitness accounts. Four friends of a paralytic break up the roof and lower him into the presence of Jesus. Repeatedly the crowds jostle the Master. The waves beat upon the boat which carries Him and His disciples across the Sea of Galilee and threaten to swamp it (4:37). In preparation for feeding the 5,000 Jesus orders that the people sit in groups "on the green grass" (6:39). On the mount of transfiguration the voice of God the Father thunders from the cloud, "This is my beloved Son, listen to him" (9:7). Again and again the reader is caught up in the drama of the narrative and experiences the sensation of "you are there."

Contemporary individuals are also attracted by the humanness of Christ as He appears in the Gospel of Mark. They find it easier to identify with a God who demonstrates human characteristics. Jesus was not merely concerned with issues of theology and ethics. He was moved with compassion or pity when He observed the physical needs of people and did something about them. This pity is noted specifically in connection with His healing the leper and feeding the multitudes (1:41; 6:34; 8:2), but He must have been similarly affected when He performed other miracles. Jesus' humanness is demonstrated also by His indignation (3:5; 8:2; 10:14), His distress and sorrow (14:33,34), and the fact that He died (15:37). Numerous other illustrations could be given, but they will become evident in our study of the text of the book.

One must be careful, however, not to put too much stress on the humanity of Christ, for Mark clearly portrays Him as God. The Father bore witness to this fact at the baptism and the Transfiguration (1:11; 9:7) and the demons attested it (1:24; 3:11; 5:7). Jesus claimed it (2:5-11; 13:32; 14:62) and the centurion recognized it (15:39). As a human being He could reveal the love and concern of God to humanity and could suffer the penalty that mankind deserved for its sin. As Deity, as the infinite One, He could pay the penalty for the sin of *all* mankind.

Authorship

From the beginning of the second century, early church leaders were unanimous in speaking of Mark as the author of the second Gospel. In fact, they represent the apostle John as teaching that not only did Mark write the Gospel but he did so under the influence of or as the interpreter of Peter. Thus the book gains apostolic authority or sanction. There is also a tradition that Mark wrote in Rome after the departure (generally understood to mean the death) of Peter and Paul there. If this is true, Mark wrote after A.D. 65. Indications within the book lead us to conclude that the destruction of Jerusalem (A.D. 70) had not yet occurred. Hence the book must have been written about 67 or 68. One would not expect a tradition of Mark's authorship to develop if it were not true; he was after all a minor figure. It is significant that no worthy alternate proposal as to authorship has been made.

Internal evidence for any of these conclusions is minimal. As to Roman origin, it is often noted that Mark 15:21 names Simon of Cyrene, father of Alexander and Rufus, as bearer of the cross of Christ and that

Rufus and his mother were living in Rome at the time the epistle to the Romans was written (Rom. 16:13). If one accepts identification of the Rufus of Mark 15:21 and Romans 16:13, as many do, Mark's inclusion of this detail would have had special significance for the Roman church. Moreover, Latinisms in Mark often are pointed out. Transliterations of Latin words into Greek are more frequent than in the other Gospels. Certainly the contents of the Gospel reflect an eyewitness to the events; if he was not Peter, he had to be one of the other apostles. Commentators frequently suggest that the young man who fled when Jesus was arrested was Mark (Mark 14:51,52), but one cannot be sure of such an identification.

As to Mark's biography, it is known that he had a home in Jerusalem. And it is suggested that the upper room of that home was used for the Last Supper and also for the Pentecostal gathering. John Mark, a cousin of Barnabas (Col. 4:10), joined Barnabas and Saul on the first missionary journey and ministered with them in Cyprus (Acts 13:5), but left the party in Perga and returned to Jerusalem (Acts 13:13). At the time of his second journey Paul refused to take John Mark along again (apparently feeling he was too undependable). Barnabas took Mark off on another mission to Cyprus and Paul took Silas and went to Asia Minor and Greece. Mark showed up in Rome during Paul's imprisonment there and sent greetings to the Colossians and Philemon (Col. 4:10; Philem. 24). In 1 Peter 5:13 Peter refers to Mark as "my son"; perhaps he was Peter's understudy as Timothy was Paul's. At any rate, Paul spoke well of Mark in 2 Timothy 4:11 and desired his company during his last days on earth. Whatever Mark's failures earlier in life, he had subsequently proved himself.

Mark's Message

Students of the Gospel of Mark frequently call attention to the similarity of the book to Peter's sermon to the Gentiles in Acts 10:34-43. They see the Gospel as a "catechetical expansion" which consciously or unconsciously filled in the outline of Peter's sermon. Peter started with the ministry of John the Baptist, proceeded to note the anointing of Jesus at the baptism, and then moved on to Jesus' ministry in Galilee, Judea, and Jerusalem, and concluded with His death and resurrection. Mark followed this same general pattern in composing his gospel. Evidently he intended to present the story of Jesus Christ as good news. Basic to this good news or gospel was his emphasis on Jesus as the

Servant of Jehovah. The key verse is commonly considered to be 10:45: "For even the Son of Man did not come to be served, but to serve, and to give his life a ransom for many" (NIV). The first half of the verse applies especially to the first half of the book, down to 8:30, where emphasis is on the ministry of Christ. The latter half of the verse relates to the portion after 8:31, which focuses on the Passion of Christ.

Mark's message would have had a special appeal to Gentiles in general and Roman readers in particular. During the Passion Week when Jesus cleansed the temple, He indicated it was to be "a house of prayer for all the nations" (11:17). And when Jesus uttered His prophetic discourse, He specified that the gospel some day would be preached to "all nations" (13:10). Mark makes fewer allusions to the Old Testament than the other Gospel writers, interprets Aramaic words, explains numerous items of Jewish law, customs, and geography, and has numerous Latinisms. Many early church leaders, including Irenaeus, Clement of Alexandria, and Jerome, specifically stated that Mark wrote for Roman readers.

Outline

There are numerous ways of outlining the Book of Mark. The following outline centers on the theme of Jesus as the Servant of Jehovah.

I. Preparation of the Servant (1:1-13)
   A. Introduction of Jesus (1:1-8)
   B. Preparation of Jesus (1:9-13)
II. Proclamation of the Servant (1:14–8:30)
   A. Launching of ministry (1:14-45)
   B. Beginning of opposition (2:1–3:6)
   C. Organization of forces (3:7-35)
   D. A day of kingdom parables (4:1-41)
   E. Faith failing and triumphant (5:1-43)
   F. Beginning of discipleship (6:1-56)
   G. Tradition challenged (7:1–8:10)
   H. Sight and insight (8:11-30)
III. Passion of the Servant (8:31–16:20)
   A. Preview of passion and glory (8:31–9:29)
   B. Greatness in humble service (9:30–10:52)
   C. Jesus' kingly authority (11:1-26)

D. Temple cross-examination (11:27–12:44)
E. Prophecy and warning (13:1-37)
F. The self-sacrifice of the Servant (14:1–15:47)
G. Resurrection (16:1-20)

For Further Study

1. How is Christ presented in each of the four Gospels? For whom was each of the Gospels written? You may get help in answering these questions by reading articles in a Bible dictionary or Bible encyclopedia on the Gospels as a whole or on each of the individual Gospels.

2. What can you find in Mark's emphases or omissions that would appeal to Gentile or Roman readers?

3. If you were to highlight the geographical movement of the Gospel of Mark, how would you outline the book?

Chapter 2

Preparation of the Servant
(Mark 1:1-13)

Introduction of Jesus (1:1-8)

Verse 1 introduces the book tersely and simply. It is like a title or caption. One can almost see a herald striding on stage, playing a fanfare, and announcing a drama: "Beginning of the gospel of Jesus Christ, Son of God." The terseness of the statement epitomizes the whole Gospel and creates the attitude, "Let's plunge in."

Taken as a title of the book, this verse indicates that the topic of Mark's literary production is the "gospel of Jesus Christ." "Gospel" cannot refer to the book Mark is introducing; it never does apply to a book in the New Testament. Rather, it designates the good news of salvation. Furthermore, if verse 1 is a title, then "of Jesus Christ" must be taken to mean "concerning Jesus Christ." If it were applied to teachings belonging to or uttered by Jesus Christ, it would be inappropriate because His teachings do not appear in any degree of fullness in the book. "Beginning" of the gospel implies continuation and certainly has to do with all that "Jesus began both to do and teach" (Acts 1:1).

The good news concerned "Jesus Christ." Jesus is His personal name (Matt. 1:21) and is the Greek form of the Hebrew *Joshua*, which means "Jehovah is salvation" or "Jehovah provides salvation." Christ is the Greek equivalent to the Hebrew *Messiah*, meaning "the anointed one," God's agent for establishment of His kingdom on earth. Though "Son of God" is not in some manuscripts, the textual evidence for inclusion is strong and the words should be retained. The significance of the term is no doubt the same here as elsewhere in Scripture—He is coequal with the Father as the second person of the Godhead. Though Mark focuses on the servanthood and humanity of Jesus, the deity of

Savior, the coming King, the Son of God. This verse is to be contrasted with Mathew 1:1 in the lack of a genealogy, with Luke 1:1 in the lack of a prologue, and with John 1:1 in the lack of a discourse on the deity of Christ.

The ministry of John the Baptist. The introduction of Jesus or the preparation for Him continues with a statement about the ministry of John the Baptist. Neither the coming and sacrifice of Christ nor the preparation for His coming by John the Baptist was unanticipated. In fact, Christ's provision for mankind's sin problem had been in the mind of God even before the Creation (e.g., Eph. 1:4). And the appearance of a forerunner of the Messiah had been announced some 700 years earlier in the prophets. The first part of Mark's Old Testament quotation came from Malachi 3:1 (v. 2) and the second part from Isaiah 40:3 (v. 3). The best texts of Mark 1:2 read, "Even as it stands written in Isaiah the prophet." Some have jumped on Mark for an inaccuracy here but apparently the reference to Isaiah is what chiefly occupied his mind. "As it stands written" is a translation of the Greek perfect tense and refers to that which was written and still remains. The living, abiding quality of the Old Testament is implied in this reference. Moreover, the fact that the prophecy is recognized and the fulfillment of it noted testifies to the validity and inspiration of Scripture.

It is clear from verse 2 that the prophecy is spoken directly to the Messiah and involves a personal preparation for His coming ("before your face," "before you"). The imagery here refers to the practice of Oriental monarchs of sending ahead a herald to announce their coming and to fill the minds of their subjects with anticipation of the big event. To prepare the way or make the paths straight for an Oriental potentate involved more than mere psychological preparation, however. Valleys had to be filled, hills leveled, and the road straightened as much as possible (see Isa. 40:3,4). Such phraseology could be applied to preparation for Christ only in a symbolic sense. His kingdom was to be spiritual in nature and preparation for its coming would have to involve repentance—"Impenitence raises the mountains of obstruction" (Lenski, p. 27).

"John the Baptizer [present participle] came into the wilderness, preaching a baptism of repentance for the forgiveness of sins."[1] John was so well known for the function of baptizing that it actually became a part

---

[1]Translations of Scripture in this commentary are the author's own unless otherwise specified.

of his name. The wilderness where he preached was clearly the wilderness of Judea, because people from Jerusalem and the other towns of Judea went out to him (v. 5). The region in question would have been the dry and virtually unpopulated area extending east to the Jordan and the Dead Sea from a line drawn through Jerusalem and Hebron. Of course his baptism occurred in the Jordan, not far north of where it empties into the Dead Sea. His "preaching" might better be translated "proclaiming as a herald"—appropriate terminology for his activity predicted in verses 2 and 3.

At first glance verse 4 might seem to teach that baptism in some sense secures forgiveness from sin. By way of answer, it should be observed that nowhere in Scripture is there a hint that baptism saves. Moreover, as is clear in this verse, baptism is accompanied by repentance, which in the Greek connotes not a mere sorrow for sin but a fundamental change of mind or heart. The same root word is used in 1 Thessalonians 1:9, where it refers to a turning to God from idols—a complete change of direction from paganism to Christianity, from sin to righteousness. "*For* [Greek *eis*] the forgiveness of sins" is also susceptible to a different translation: "*because of* the forgiveness of sins." Interestingly this interpretation is confirmed by the first-century A.D. Jewish historian Josephus who comments that John required repentance as a prerequisite to baptism: ". . . and so to come to baptism; for that washing [with water] would be acceptable to him, if they made use of it, not in order to the putting away [or the remission] of some sins [only] but for the purification of the body; supposing still that the soul was thoroughly purified beforehand by righteousness" (*Antiquities of the Jews* XVIII.v.2).

In verse 5 Mark depicts "all" the populace of Judea going out to John. Admittedly this is an exaggeration, as is his use of "all" on other occasions. But one should not discount the claim too heavily. Among the crowds that flocked to John's baptism were representatives of all classes: Pharisees and Sadducees (Matt. 3:7), tax collectors (Luke 3:12), and soldiers (Luke 3:14). Josephus in the reference noted above shows the effectiveness of John's ministry and the great influence he had over the people. In fact, years later Paul found a group of John's disciples in faraway Ephesus (Acts 19:3). The magnetic drawing power of this man of God must have been great indeed because multitudes came out into the Christ is as important to him as it is to the apostle John in his Gospel.

To summarize, this book is about the good news concerning the wilderness to him. It is remarkable enough when the masses flock to hear a religious leader who comes into their midst; it is even more noteworthy when they seek him out in a remote place at great inconvenience or even hardship to themselves. The imperfect tenses in verse 5 add great vividness to the account. The people *kept going out* in a continual procession and *kept on being baptized,* successively, one after the other, "openly confessing their sins."

The physical appearance and diet of John the Baptist are indicated in verse 6. Clothed in the coarsest fashion, he wore a loose robe woven from camel's hair and bound at the waist with a leather belt. The belt was especially useful to the lower-class person because his garment could be tucked up in it for rapid walking or hard work. Since no sandals are mentioned, it is possible he wore none. John's attire recalls that of Elijah (2 Kings 1:8) or the prophets in general (Zech. 13:4). John's diet was also very simple: locusts and wild honey. Some today try to identify the locusts John ate as carob beans, eaten by cattle and the very poor. But it is almost certain that the reference is to the insect, which was allowed for food (Lev. 11:22). Locusts were dried or roasted or ground up and mixed with flour and water and baked into cakes. Wild honey could be found in many of the fissures and clefts in the limestone rocks in the wilderness of Judea.

In verse 7 John "proclaimed as a herald" the coming of the Messiah. The use of the present tense in "comes" shows that with prophetic insight John sees Jesus as already come. He is a man of great humility, not even considering himself worthy to tie or untie the thong of Jesus' sandal—a task of a menial slave. His entire ministry was to point to the Lamb of God (John 1:36). Truly John was one of the world's most humble men. But humility does not connote weakness; it has been called "controlled strength." Certainly there was nothing weak or fearful about John the Baptist. He was equally capable of condemning the religious establishment (the Pharisees and Sadducees, Matt. 3:7) and the political establishment (Herod Antipas, Mark 6:18).

As John compares the difference between his person and that of Jesus, so he contrasts his work with that of the Master. John baptizes in connection with water; Jesus shall baptize in connection with the Holy Spirit. "A divinely appointed man may apply water in a sacrament; only the Son of God can pour out the Holy Spirit, and even he only after completing his redemptive work and then ascending to heaven" (Lenski, p. 40). This baptism would bring with it a new enduement of spiritual power (Acts 1:8). The age of the Messiah was expected to be accompanied by an outpouring of the power of the Holy Spirit (Joel 2:28,29; Acts 1:5; 2:4, 16-21). For all John's humility and his apparent insignificance when compared with Jesus Christ, he was one of the world's truly great men. Jesus declared him to be the last and greatest of the prophets and the greatest man who ever had been born (Luke 7:24-28; 16:16). Moreover, he is the only one of whom it is said in Scripture that he was filled with the Spirit from birth (Luke 1:5).

Preparation of Jesus (1:9-13)

Baptism of Jesus. "In those days," when the ministry of John was at its height, Jesus came from Nazareth in Galilee, where He had grown up in peaceful seclusion. He was now about thirty years of age. Matthew tells us that Jesus made the journey from Galilee for the purpose of being baptized (3:13). Baptism "in the Jordan" probably occurred at a ford not far from Jericho. The full significance of Jesus' baptism can only be guessed at. Certainly He was not a sinner who needed to repent under the preaching of John and be baptized as a symbol of cleansing and a break with an old life to enter a new life of holiness. At the minimum it signifies that He was identifying Himself with sinners and beginning His redemptive work. Shortly after this John called Him the "Lamb of God" (John 1:36) which alludes to His sacrifice for sin. Jesus' willingness to become the Savior is clearly evident in the various accounts of the baptism in the Gospels. His humility is also evident, not only in submitting to baptism at the hands of John, but also in letting all others go first. He was baptized after "all the people had been baptized" (Luke 3:21).

"And while he was going up out of the water, immediately he saw the heavens rent asunder and the Spirit like a dove coming down on him." At a dramatic moment like this, with the heavens split apart, one would expect ten legions of angels to descend, but instead only a dove came down. At the beginning of Christ's public ministry the heavens are torn open; at the end of His substitutionary work on the cross the veil in the temple is torn apart (15:38). The descent of the dove is followed by the voice of the Father: "Thou art My Beloved Son, in Thee I am well-pleased" (NASB). The Spirit and the Father put their stamp of approval on the Saviorhood of Christ. The voice of the Father was directed to the Son. The dove evidently was visible to John the Baptist because he mentions it (John 1:32). In verse 1 Mark spoke of Jesus as Son of God; in verse 11 the Father calls Him Son.

Temptation of Jesus. Right after the mountaintop experience at the baptism ("immediately"), Jesus descended into the valley of temptation. Mountaintop experiences were designed for the Son of man, as for modern human beings, as preparation for the valleys. The language of verse 12 is very forceful: "The Spirit drives him out into the wilderness." The Holy Spirit compelled Him to go out to the encounter. In 1 John 3:8 we read a very instructive statement: "The reason the Son of God appeared was to destroy the works of the devil" (RSV). That being the case, a conflict with the devil should be expected at the beginning of Christ's ministry. The "wilderness" is traditionally the area near ancient Jericho; and the Mount of Temptation is identified with a precipitous rock that rises to a height of 1200-1500 feet. High on the side facing Jericho one may still see remains of an early monastery built on that sacred site.

The temptation narrative in Mark is compressed into verse 13 and the forms of temptation are omitted. Details unique to this account are the use of "Satan" (one who opposes) rather than "the Devil," and the information that Jesus was "with wild beasts," indicating His aloneness. If indeed Mark wrote for the Romans, the fact that Jesus was safe from wild beasts in the wilderness might have made a special impression on them. Romans were accustomed to seeing men engage in ferocious wild-beast hunts in the Roman arena. Imagine one who suffered no threat from them, even in their wild habitat! Since "tempted" is in the imperfect tense, it indicates continuation of the temptation throughout the forty days, with the special forms of temptation noted in the other Gospels undoubtedly coming at the end of that time. Mark only implies Jesus' victory in the contest with Satan. Subsequently the angels "were ministering" (imperfect tense, indicating continued action) to Him, no doubt providing food and drink among other things.

Before leaving this first major division of the book, it will be instructive to note two major thoughts: inferences concerning the Trinity and the focus of attention on Christ. First, as to Trinitarian relationships, in verse 8 the active agent is Christ, who has power over the Holy Spirit; in verse 11 God the Father is the active agent, indicating His pleasure with the Son; in verse 12, the Holy Spirit is the active agent, driving Christ into the wilderness to face the temptation. Second, Christ is the central figure of the passage. In verse 1 the author bears witness to Him; in verses 2-8, the prophets and John the Baptist focus attention on Him; in verses 9-11, John, the Holy Spirit, and the Father center their attention on Him; in verses 12-13, Satan, wild beasts, and the angels all throw the spotlight on Him.

For Further Study

1. What geographical notations appear in Mark 1:1-13? Why are they significant?

2. Make a comparative study of the baptism of John in the Gospels. Make observations concerning his biography and his character.

3. Make a comparative study of the temptation of Jesus as recorded in the Gospels. Note the strategy of Satan and the response of Jesus.

4. Compare the prophecies concerning John the Baptist alluded to in the early chapters of the Gospels.

Chapter 3

Launching of Ministry
(Mark 1:14-45)

Mark moves directly from the temptation of Jesus to His Galilean ministry. "After John was imprisoned" signals the end of the preparatory work of John. Now Jesus may move forward with His distinctive preaching. Evidently it was Mark's purpose to concentrate on that part of Christ's ministry when He held the field alone. He skips over the first miracle of turning water into wine (John 2:1-2), the entire early Judean ministry of Christ (about a year in duration) when John and Jesus carried on their work not far apart (John 3:25-36), the return to Galilee through Samaria (John 4), healing the nobleman's son at Capernaum, and the return to Jerusalem (possibly for the Passover, John 5:1). While Jesus was out of Galilee on the latter occasion, John was imprisoned. Thus it could now be said, "Jesus came into Galilee." The part of Jesus' ministry that Mark narrates covers about two years.[1]

"The gospel of God" is the preferred reading in verse 14 and apparently refers to good news from God. As Jesus preached this good news, He announced "the time [season] has been fulfilled," the season of preparation has been completed; "the kingdom of God is at hand," the kingdom which God establishes and over which He rules is at hand. In fact, His hearers might enter this kingdom by repenting and believing in the gospel. John had called for repentance, a complete about-face, a fundamental change of mind and heart; Jesus now adds belief (a complete trust or repose) in the gospel. John had preached repentance as a preparation for the coming of Jesus. Jesus now comes to present Himself and calls for their implicit faith in the good news, apparently good news

[1]For a fuller narrative of the life of Christ, see Howard F. Vos, *Beginnings in the Life of Christ* (Chicago: Moody Press, 1975).

concerning Himself (cf. Mark 1:1). If they wished to enter the kingdom, they would have to render obedience to the Messiah-king—to receive His person and His message.

Four fishermen called (1:16-20). As Jesus launches His ministry He needs helpers. Those whom He calls should be capable people and individuals who already have a high degree of dedication to Him. Christian workers often make a big mistake when they base messages on this passage. They call modern men and women to place their faith in Christ and then to forsake all and follow Christ immediately as these fishermen did. But it should be remembered that these men did not follow Christ without considerable preparation. Peter and Andrew were, first of all, disciples of John the Baptist (John 1:35-42). Second, John had pointed them to Christ and they had followed Him for an extended period in the previous year. Third, they had been present at the first miracle (John 2:2) and had been with the Master for an extended period of time before returning to their fishing business. Fourth, as for James and John, from comparison of Mark 15:40 and John 19:25, many infer that the mother of James and John, Salome, was the sister of the Virgin Mary. Therefore James and John would have been cousins of Jesus. Even if this is not the case, James and John were partners in the fishing business with Peter and Andrew (Luke 5:10-11) and would have had considerable opportunity to learn about Jesus from them. And all four of them were tremendously impressed by the miraculous catch of fish (Luke 5:1-11).

Furthermore, there is no evidence that these four fishermen completely forsook all their wealth when they followed Jesus. James and John left their boats and the business in the hands of their father and the hired help (Mark 1:20). Since they were partners, Zebedee may have managed the affairs of Peter and Andrew also. Or possibly Peter had a manager who looked after the business. He continued to maintain a house in Capernaum, which seems to have served as apostolic headquarters. This presupposes some kind of income. In calling the four fishermen to follow Him, Jesus does so in language they would understand: "Come, follow me, and I will make you fishers of men." As they had caught fish and brought them to shore for human use, so now by means of the gospel net they are to try to bring men and women to Christ.

Sabbath healings (1:21-34). After the disciples responded to Jesus' call they accompanied Him into nearby Capernaum, their home and His headquarters after His rejection at Nazareth (Luke 4:16-31). The town was located on the northwestern shore of the Sea of Galilee. Not long after, perhaps the next day, Jesus went to the regular Sabbath service in the synagogue. There He astounded the congregation because He taught with authority and independent judgment rather than as the scribes, who simply quoted the decisions of earlier rabbis.

While in the synagogue He encountered a man under the influence of an unclean spirit, who presumably would have created no disturbance under normal circumstances. But confronted by the presence of the holy One, the spirit went on the defensive and blurted out Jesus' true identity. "Demons believe and tremble" (James 2:19) even when men are too blind to recognize Him. Jesus did not accept this witness because people were not yet ready for such forthright declarations. "Be muzzled, and come out of him," Jesus commanded. The spirit threw the man into convulsions and came out of him, causing the congregation to be amazed and leading to a spread of Jesus' fame in the surrounding region. On this occasion there was no charge of His having broken the Sabbath by healing on that day, as frequently would be the case later on. Earlier Jesus had won a victory over Satan at the temptation; now He wins a victory over Satan's kingdom.

After the morning service, Jesus went to the house of Simon Peter and Andrew. James and John accompanied Him, probably for a lunch; therefore all four disciples were present for another miracle. As the group entered the house, Jesus was promptly informed that Peter's mother-in-law lay sick with a burning fever, and Luke makes it clear that those present requested Him to help her (Luke 4:38). Mark offers graphic details: Jesus went to the sufferer, took her by the hand, lifted her up, the fever left, and she ministered to them. Evidently a real miracle had occurred, because not only did the fever leave but she was immediately well enough to serve her guests. The service was minimal that day, however, because it was still the Sabbath. To those who argue for the celibacy of Peter, it must be noted that this passage clearly speaks of his mother-in-law. Moreover, his wife apparently was still alive because 1 Corinthians 9:5 later refers to the fact that she accompanied Peter in his ministry, at least part of the time.

At the end of the Sabbath, "at sundown," the people of Capernaum sought Jesus' healing touch on the sick and demon-possessed. No doubt they waited until the Sabbath was over so they would not be guilty of breaking the law or infringing on rabbinical pronouncements, which prohibited work or burden-bearing on the Sabbath. That Jesus could exorcise demons would have been known all over town after the morning service was over. No doubt news of restoration of Peter's mother-in-law likewise had spread widely. Jews of the New Testament period did not go far on the Sabbath, but it may be supposed that at least both Peter's wife and her mother would have gone out of doors after the miracle occurred. Excavations of the fishermen's quarter in Capernaum show how closely houses were packed together. One needed only to step outside and chat with a neighbor. Within a short time anything said would have been known all over the village. The townspeople "brought," *kept bearing* or carrying to Jesus in a steady procession, the sick and demon-possessed. The "whole city," the sick, interested loved ones, and the curious, were massed outside the door of Peter's house. This detail appears only here in the Gospels. No doubt the experience would have made a profound impression on Peter who presumably furnished Mark with information for his Gospel. Reference to Jesus' healing "many who were sick" does not imply there were some He could not cure but only that those healed were numerous. Matthew specifically states that He healed all the sick who came to Him on this occasion (8:16). Although the Gospels record only thirty-five specific miracles of Jesus, there are several references of this sort that imply a large number of miracles. As in the case of the synagogue demoniac, Jesus did not permit the demons (evidently distinguished from the personality of the demon-possessed) to bear witness of Him. He wanted a willing, joyous witness of His person rather than a grudging acknowledgment.

A Galilean tour (1:35-45). After a long and tiring Saturday, Jesus rose very early on Sunday, perhaps between three and four in the morning, and went out to an uninhabited place to pray. The plain along the shore of the Sea of Galilee is so narrow that He would not have had to go far to find a lonely spot in the hills. It is instructive to the modern Christian to know that the Son of God felt the need for fellowship with the Father before embarking on an expanded ministry. What the disciples thought when they discovered Jesus missing is not known. Certainly the townspeople were worried about losing Him and wanted to keep Him for themselves (see Luke 4:42). Simon led a search party as they literally *pursued closely* or *tracked out* the Master. Already the importance of Simon is in evidence in the book; in 1:16 Andrew is described as the brother of Simon; in verse 30 his mother-in-law was healed; in verse 36 he led the group of disciples and spoke for them. "All" the people of Capernaum were looking for Him, perhaps already camped out at Peter's doorstep.

Fired with a sense of mission, Jesus refuses to settle down in Capernaum but insists on going to nearby village towns or country towns—places like Bethsaida and Chorazin, which were more than mere villages but not really cities. It was to "preach" (not primarily to heal and cast out demons) that He "came forth"—probably a reference to His leaving the Father and the glories of heaven. Mark is content with a terse comment (v. 39) concerning Jesus' first Galilean tour. It must have been comprehensive ("throughout all Galilee"), and involved healing as well as the accompanying casting out of demons.

While on this Galilean tour Jesus met a leper. Evidently this man had heard about the miracles Jesus had performed and came seeking healing. He had no doubt that Jesus could heal, saying only "If you will, you can make me clean" (v. 40). Mark adds the graphic details that Jesus was "moved with compassion" and He did the unbelievable—touching the untouchable and healing the incurable. Then He "commanded with sternness" and "cast him out immediately" with the order that the healed man show himself to the priest to meet the requirements of the Mosaic law for cleansing (Lev. 14). We can presume Jesus was urgent with the leper so that the report would not precede the man to the priest and therefore Jesus' enemies would not have a chance to deny either the man's former state or the reality of the healing. The leper's appearance before the priests would indeed be a wonderful "testimony" to the person and work of Christ.

But unfortunately the man was so overcome with the joy of being healed that he disobeyed Jesus and "began to publish it much," and thus brought to an abrupt end Jesus' town ministry. The Master was so thronged by the curious seekers and the infirm that He was forced to carry on His work in uninhabited places. At the beginning of the chapter the "forerunner" chose to preach in the desert places of Judea and multitudes came out to hear him. At the end of the chapter the Messiah was forced to preach in the uninhabited places of Galilee because He was so thronged in the cities, and crowds also came out of the cities to hear Him. In verse 12 Jesus was driven into the wilderness by the Holy Spirit for testing; in verse 45 He was driven into the wilderness by crowds of seekers.

For Further Study

1. Study time and place notations in Mark 1:14-45. What do they contribute to the development of the section?

2. What problems confronted Jesus in these verses and how did He handle them?

3. Chart the reactions to Jesus in this passage as follows: reaction, person or group reacting, reason for the reaction.

4. What changes did Jesus bring about in these verses? (E.g., change in occupation, physical condition, etc.)

5. What centers of life did Jesus touch? (E.g., occupation, the physical, mental, spiritual, etc.)

Chapter 4

Beginning of Opposition
(Mark 2:1 – 3:6)

Jesus had effectively launched His ministry. The whole of Galilee was stirred with excitement over His preaching and His miracles. His increasing popularity inevitably would threaten the religious establishment. Threatened individuals normally respond with attacks of their own. In this section appears the beginning and rising crescendo of opposition. Starting with questioning, it eventuates in a plot to kill Him (3:6).

The uncovered roof (2:1-2). After an indefinite period spent in itinerant Galilean ministry ("some days," 2:1), Jesus returned to Capernaum, where He had experienced the first flush of popularity. As soon as the word spread that He was "at home," crowds began to gather. Whether "at home" refers to a place where He had lived after the move from Nazareth or the house of Peter cannot be determined with certainty. In any case, the crowd was packed in so tight that there was no access through the door. On this occasion there is no record of miracles being performed; Jesus "was speaking the word." When four men arrived carrying a paralyzed friend on a bed pallet, they found it impossible to get the man to Jesus. So they resorted to the unorthodox plan of lowering him through the roof. While Jesus continued to speak, they apparently ascended the customary outside stairway to the flat roof and broke up or "dug out" the top layer of grass and clay and then pulled up the clay tiles (Luke 5:19) which lay on the roof beams and lowered the man to the feet of Christ. "When Jesus saw their faith," the faith of both the paralytic and those who carried him, He said, "Son, your sins are forgiven." To us, this may seem like a strange response on the part of Christ to an evident physical need. But Hiebert observes, "The proce-

dure of Jesus was in harmony with the current Jewish view that forgiveness of sins must precede physical recovery. The rabbis said, 'There is
no sick man healed of his sickness until all his sins have been forgiven
him'" (p. 64).

Jesus' audience was not all friendly. "Certain scribes" (v. 6) apparently were watching His every move and were collecting charges against
Him. Luke says in the parallel passage that Pharisees and doctors of the
law had come out of every town of Galilee and even from Judea and
Jerusalem and converged on Capernaum (Luke 5:17). Presumably this
happened while Jesus was away on His Galilean tour. Opposition of the
Judean establishment was already quite advanced as a result of Jesus'
extended earlier ministry there (John 5:18).

These men did not openly contest with Him but reasoned "within
themselves." Assuming that Jesus was a mere man, the scribes concluded that He was guilty of blasphemy because He claimed the ability
to forgive sins—an act generally recognized to be a work of God alone.
Almost as if to say, "I am not a mere man but possess also the power of
omniscience," Jesus "realized in his spirit" what they were thinking and
confronted them directly and specifically with their thoughts. He asked
them whether it was easier to claim to forgive sins or to claim to heal this
man, for both would require the power of God.

"But that you may know . . . by doing that which is capable of
being put to the proof, I will vindicate My right and power to do that
which, in its very nature, is incapable of being proved" (Maclear, p. 64).
"Son of man" is the term Jesus commonly chose to apply to Himself. It
appears fourteen times in Mark. Though Son of God from eternity, He
became Son of man in time and subsequently the Second Adam or
second head of the race. The term appeared in Daniel 7:13 and during
the Intertestamental period came to be a designation of the Messiah. In
obedience to the command of Jesus the paralytic "immediately," showing the instantaneous nature of the cure, arose, rolled up his pallet (little
more than a mat) and walked away. The scribes had no comment;
presumably their opposition grew more intense. The crowd was
"amazed and glorified God" as they acknowledged an operation of
supernatural power. But there was no comment about the forgiveness of
sins.

The call of Levi (2:3-17). Apparently right after the crowd dispersed
following the healing of the paralytic Jesus went out to walk along the
shore of the Sea of Galilee. As He did so, "the crowd kept coming to him

and he kept teaching them." The imperfect tenses indicate continued action and imply a situation in which groups of people came and went around the busy waterfront. "As he was passing by he saw Levi." He was probably known by this name among his Jewish acquaintances but may have changed his name after his call. Henceforth he seems to have been known as Matthew (meaning "gift of God"). In three of the apostolic lists, Matthew appears next to Thomas, also called Didymus, which means "twin," and on this basis some have felt that the two were brothers. His home was probably Capernaum, and his father's name was Alphaeus, although likely not the same as the father of James the Younger (Less).

Jesus found Levi sitting at the tax office collecting customs or dues. Probably in the service of Herod Antipas, he collected duties on goods which passed through this busy center to Tyre, Damascus, Jerusalem, and elsewhere. Jesus called Levi to become one of His disciples and he responded immediately. Whether or not he had any spiritual preparation in having heard John the Baptist or Jesus' message from another, we cannot determine. Certainly he was familiar with all the stir that had centered around Jesus and His message in previous weeks.

From Mark's Gospel it is not clear what is going on in 2:15-17, but from the parallel passage in Luke 5 we learn that after answering Jesus' call Levi gave a great feast for his new Master. It might have been something of a farewell to the old life or his way of seeking to expose his circle of acquaintances to Jesus. This crowd would not have frequented the synagogue where Jesus preached. "As he reclined at table in his house" probably means, "As Jesus reclined at table in Levi's house." "Many tax collectors and sinners were reclining with Jesus and his disciples." The implication is that Levi was wealthy because much room would have been required for the dining couches on which guests reclined around a table. "Many who followed him" probably refers to many tax collectors who followed Jesus. Tax collectors would have been Jews, presumably in the employ of Herod Antipas (son of Herod the Great, who ruled Galilee and Perea), and were hated for their cooperation with Roman oppressors, and for their unjust or illegal exactions. "Sinners" could refer to persons of low morals or individuals who demonstrated little respect for the law or the rigorous legal system spun out by the Scribes and Pharisees.

It is possible that some of the same "Scribes and Pharisees" who had sought to find evidence against Jesus at the healing of the paralytic were now hounding Him again. We see a slight advance in the intensity of the opposition here. Instead of being silent, as on the previous occasion, they are now vocal. But they do not yet launch a frontal attack. Rather, they go to Jesus' disciples and try to discredit Him in their eyes by criticizing Him for eating with tax collectors and sinners. As proper persons themselves, they did not enter Levi's house, and possibly after the meal a group of disciples stood outside chatting.

At any rate, Jesus heard about the criticism and answered His critics directly. He started out with an axiomatic truth: "Those who are healthy do not need a doctor, but the sick." Then He concluded: "I did not come to call the righteous, but sinners." Here is a statement of His mission. It might be paraphrased, "I did not come to call individuals who regard themselves as righteous or whom society regards as upright, but I came to call those who recognize that they are sinners and in need of a Savior." Of course one cannot win sinners if he never goes near them.

The fasting question (2:18-22). Opposition to Jesus now takes a different tack. In the first instance it was directed against Jesus but was not verbalized. Then opponents verbalized their criticism of Jesus but voiced it to His disciples. Here they come directly to Jesus but complain about His disciples: they failed to keep fast days which devout Jews observed.

"John's disciples and the Pharisees were fasting." Though some of John's disciples (e.g., Andrew and Simon Peter) became followers of the Messiah for whom John's ministry prepared, evidently most of them continued as a body during Christ's ministry—observing the rules, fasts, and forms of prayer John had taught them. Pharisees fasted twice a week, on the second and fifth days, though the Mosaic law had prescribed a fast only on the Day of Atonement (Lev. 16:29). Perhaps Levi's feast fell on a fast day observed by both groups. If so, they would have been somewhat affronted by this merriment while they took a position of pious sobriety. Evidently representatives of the two groups came to Jesus to inquire about His practices. Presumably the Pharisees were rankled by Jesus, who did not play ball by their game plan. The disciples of John may have been seeking an answer to a query. Apparently John's disciples actually raised the question (cf. Matt. 9:14) and Jesus answered them directly.

He replied both in terms of Hebrew practices and the ministry of John. "The sons of the bridal hall," the friends and companions of the bridegroom who came with him to the house of the bride for the marriage, could not be expected to fast as long as the bridegroom was present. It would be contrary to all social practices and would be an affront to the bridegroom. Moreover, John the Baptist had pointed to Jesus as the bridegroom and had classified himself as a friend of the bridegroom (John 3:29), in whose presence one should rejoice. In Mark 1:20 the tone suddenly changes with a prediction of the removal of the bridegroom—the first recorded hint in Jesus' public teaching of His passion.

Having given a general answer to the question posed, Jesus next moves on to present a general principle. Here as on so many other occasions, He does a marvelous job of talking to people on the level where they live and of presenting truth through the homely expressions of everyday life. The basic idea in verses 21 and 22 is clear; the application of truth takes a little more effort. One does not patch an old garment with new unshrunk material. If he should, when he washes the garment the new piece of cloth will shrink and create a much worse tear. Likewise, when an animal skin is used in the process of fermenting wine it is stretched to the limit; if new wine should be put into one of these old stretched skins, it will burst the skin and the wine will be spilled. These verses seem to argue that Christ and His teachings are not merely to be added to an old system; His ministry is something entirely new. Burdick puts the idea well, "Thus it is not possible to confine to the structure of the old legalism the vitality of the new experience produced by faith in Christ" (p. 993).

Lord of Sabbath (2:23-28). One Sabbath Jesus and His disciples were walking through the grain fields and began to pick the grain as they went. Evidently the fields were on the edge of town because there was no accusation of breaking the Sabbath by traveling too far, and they were within sight of the fastidious Pharisees who would never have broken rabbinical controls on Sabbath travel. As a matter of fact a Sabbath day's journey was 3,000 feet. The picture we get, then, is of the disciples walking on a footpath through the grain on the edge of a town. As they did so, they picked a few heads of grain and rubbed them in their hands and ate them. The grain could have been wheat or barley; but since they rubbed it in their hands (Luke 6:1), it must have been wheat, for one would not separate barley in that way. The time of the year would have been a week or two after Passover, probably sometime in May. Evidently Jesus and His disciples were hungry (v. 25) and in such cases the law permitted picking grain in a neighbor's field (Deut. 23:25) so there was no question here of theft. But the rabbis had decided that picking any grain was reaping, and rubbing it free from the head was threshing. Hence the Pharisees accused Jesus' disciples of breaking the Sabbath. Again the attack was oblique; they did not question Him but the action of His disciples.

"Did you never read what David did?" By way of answer, Jesus hit the Pharisees at their strongest point, the knowledge of Scripture. The Pharisees were immensely proud of their grasp of Scripture, but here Christ implies that they lacked application of it or forgot parts of it when they chose. He builds on their knowledge of the Old Testament to overthrow their own arguments against Him. Could they condemn David who in a moment of great need had taken the twelve loaves of the Bread of the Presence (showbread) from the tabernacle, legally eaten only by the priests, and shared it with his men (1 Sam. 21:1-6)? The expected answer is no. Then why should they condemn Him and His followers in their need (v. 25; cf. Matt. 12:1) for a trifling infraction.

Having introduced the concept of some exception to regulations when human need requires, Jesus next proposed a more flexible approach to the Sabbath: "The sabbath was made for man, not man for the sabbath." The Sabbath was instituted for the sake of human beings, to provide for rest, recuperation, and spiritual refreshment, not to be a despot that man must serve. The arbitrary regulations of the Pharisees had made the Sabbath a burden rather than a blessing. Then He proceeded to claim that He was "lord even of the sabbath." His lordship over other things extended "even" to the Sabbath. Lordship implies administration, rule, authority to regulate, and even to set aside regulations imposed by the Pharisees. He was not claiming freedom to violate the sabbath law, but ability to interpret it. On this claim of Jesus, Hiebert significantly observes, "In the Old Testament, the Sabbath is the Lord's day; Jesus' claim to be lord of the Sabbath was an implied claim to equality with Jehovah" (p. 79).

The man with the withered hand (3:1-6). "And" connects this fifth conflict between Jesus and His opponents with the previous four and marks a climax of opposition—with a plot against His life. "He entered again into the synagogue," thought to be the synagogue in Capernaum. A man was there with "a withered hand"; the Greek indicates that it had become withered, probably from accident or disease, and was not therefore a congenital defect. "They kept watching him closely" (i.e., played the spy), with malicious intent to see if He would heal the man and violate their prescriptions for Sabbath observance and provide a basis for accusing Him. Jesus knew their thoughts and, according to Matthew 12:10, forced them to verbalize the question of whether it was lawful to heal on the Sabbath. These hard-hearted legalists did not ask, "Is it merciful?" Up to this point the man who was the object of the attention and conversation had sat quietly by. Now Jesus commands him, "Stand up in the midst," which was to stand up right where he was so all could see his pitiable condition. From the Matthew account it is clear that Jesus next proceeded to lecture His accusers, pointing out that if a sheep fell into a pit on the sabbath, they would rescue the poor animal, and that a man is worth more than a sheep. Then He turned their legal question into a question of humanity, "Is it lawful to do good on the sabbath . . . to save life?" As Lenski beautifully observes, "Deeds that are morally excellent would only grace and honor the old Jewish legal Sabbath" (p. 134). "To leave the man unhealed would be morally base—the greatest desecration of the Sabbath" (p. 135). The Pharisees were licked, but they would not admit it; "they kept silent."

What a dramatic moment! In the dead silence Jesus "looked around upon them with anger," with a piercing look of righteous indignation against evil. It must have been a withering look of judgment. Peter (who presumably furnished Mark with his information), more than any of the other disciples, would have occasion to remember the look of the Master (Luke 22:61). The look of anger (in the Greek aorist tense) was momentary; His grieving was in the present tense and continuing. Their hardness of heart was a willful resistance of the heart to divine truth. Then Jesus broke the silence. Turning to the man who stood among the seated congregation He commanded, "Stretch out your hand." In faith he obeyed and before their very eyes the flesh began to fill out the fingers and the musculature returned to its normal condition. And Jesus could not be accused of working on the Sabbath; He did not get up or touch the man but simply healed him by the force of His will.

The Pharisees were furious (Luke 6:11), and proving their hardness of heart, went out to hatch a plot with the Herodians to destroy Him. Hiebert laments, "They regarded it a terrible crime for Jesus to heal on the Sabbath, but they had no qualms about plotting murder on the Sabbath!" (p. 83). The two threatened establishments got together. The Pharisees (the religious leaders of Galilee, with power centered in the synagogue) and the Herodians (political supporters of the Herodian family, in this case Herod Antipas) both stood to lose considerably if Jesus became too popular or too powerful.

For Further Study

1. Study each incident of this section separately, noting in each the action and the reactions.
2. What is revealed of Jesus in this section?
3. What is revealed about the disciples in this section?
4. What would you forecast for Jesus' future, based on this section?

Chapter 5

Organizing of Forces
(Mark 3:7-35)

Conflicts with the Pharisees did not in any way hinder Jesus' effectiveness. The miracles He continued to perform and His teachings led to ever greater popularity with the masses. In fact, the demands on Him grew to the point where He needed additional help to carry on His ministry. Therefore He chose the twelve disciples, who would remain in an observer status for a while but later would become apprentices.

Crowds from abroad (3:7-12). After the synagogue contest, Jesus withdrew with His disciples (at least Simon, Andrew, James, John, and Matthew) to some undesignated spot near the Sea of Galilee. The reason for solitude was certainly not fear but perhaps was for rest or for a session with His disciples. Mark notes several occasions when Jesus retired from His work for prayer, rest, or conferences with His disciples (1:35; 3:7; 6:31-32; 7:24; 9:2; 14:32). At first a "great crowd" gathered from Galilee, but in time many came from regions more distant—Judea and Jerusalem, Idumea (south of Judea in southern Palestine), beyond Jordan (Perea), and Tyre and Sidon (in Phoenicia to the north). The only area not represented was Samaria. Apparently the mob almost got out of hand at times because Jesus told His disciples to keep a small boat constantly ready—presumably so He could get out in it and use it for a pulpit. Mark explains that the sick almost threatened to crush the Master as they sought to touch Him and experience His life-giving power. And again and again, whenever evil spirits in demon-possessed persons came in contact with Him, they acknowledged that He was "the Son of God." But it was His practice to rebuke them severely that they should not make Him known. In Scripture God has ordained that only those who have experienced divine grace shall witness or testify of

Christ and His saving power. He does not employ either evil spirits or the unfallen ones (angels) as witnesses.

Appointing the Twelve (3:13-19). The pressure of meeting the needs of the crowds was staggering; Jesus needed help. Furthermore, the time would come for Him to leave the scene and He must prepare others to take over the work He would leave behind. About two years remained for the Master to train them. Moreover, up to this point Jesus had seemed to stand almost alone. The followers who had gathered around Him did not form an organized body in the face of growing opposition. Such a body was now to be formed.

In preparation for this crucial event in His ministry, Jesus spent all night in prayer to the Father (Luke 6:12) on some mountain or high hill west of the Sea of Galilee. Then in the morning "he calls to himself whom he himself desired." Though many had exercised their wills in attaching themselves to His entourage, He did not now ask for volunteers. Rather, He chose certain men to constitute a special group. Evidently the call came in two stages. First he called together all His recognized followers who "went off unto him" up the hill. Then from this larger group and in their presence He "appointed twelve," literally made or constituted twelve as a separate group (see Luke 6:13). The reason for twelve generally has been taken as corresponding to the twelve patriarchs and the twelve tribes of the Old Covenant. It is important to note that first the Twelve were to be "with him," for fellowship and instruction as foundational to all service for the Master. Second, they were to preach the message committed to them, and that message would become more definitive after the death, burial, and resurrection of Christ. Then they were to have "authority to cast out demons." They would need divine authority in any contest with the forces of the evil one. No doubt the driving out of demons would on occasion serve as confirmation of their teaching. Modern disciples of Jesus should take note that fellowship with Him is of prime importance, with service in second place, and exercise of miraculous powers or gifts in third place.

Now appears the list of the Twelve. Other lists occur in the New Testament in Matthew 10:2-4; Luke 6:14-16; and Acts 1:13. In all of these Simon Peter is in first place. Andrew, James, and John appear in second, third, and fourth places, though not in the same order in all lists. Philip is in fifth place in all lists and Bartholomew, Matthew, and Thomas in sixth, seventh, and eighth places, though not always in the same order. James of Alphaeus is always in ninth place and Judas Iscariot in last place, while Simon the Zealot or Simon the Cananaean and Thaddaeus fill the other two places.

Simon was surnamed Peter and is called by his new name in the rest of the Book of Mark. This probably signifies his official function as a foundation rock in the building of the church (see Matt. 16:18; Eph. 2:20). James and John were called Boanerges or sons of thunder, perhaps because of their fiery zeal; the title seems to be a term of honor, though modern preachers often attach negative features to it. Bartholomew is presumably the Nathanael of John 1:45. Thaddeus seems also to have been called Lebbeus and Judas (of James). Simon the Cananaean is identical with Simon the Zealot in other lists. Cananaean is a transcription of the Aramaic term which means "the zealot." Simon supposedly was a former member of this Jewish nationalist party. Judas called Iscariot is probably a Hebrew term meaning "man of Kerioth," a village south of Hebron. If so, he was the only Judean in the group. This fact possibly could have led to some friction with the other disciples. He is commonly identified as the betrayer in the Gospels.

Beelzebub (3:20-27). As Jesus' popularity increases and as He throws Himself unstintingly into His ministry, His zeal is misinterpreted by relatives and foes alike. They conclude that He is somewhat mentally or emotionally unbalanced, or worse, energized by demonic power. "And he comes into a house" (i.e., home), probably refers to a return to Peter's house in Capernaum. Hardly had Jesus returned to Capernaum when the crowds gathered "again." He was mobbed as He had been earlier (2:1ff.), "so that they could not even eat bread." Evidently the crowds did not give the apostolic company a chance to relax after their journey or even time to have a meal. All this activity at his house must have made a great impression on Peter for Mark is the only Gospel writer who adds the graphic touches of the scene. Apparently people kept coming with their needs; and the reckless abandon with which Jesus threw Himself into His ministry to them led some to conclude that He was somewhat unstable emotionally.

"When his friends heard it." Evidently reference is not to the disciples because they were with Him and did not need to hear reports of what was going on. The Greek is literally "those from him," i.e., those from His home, or those who belonged to Him. Commentators and translators generally conclude that his relatives are involved. At Nazareth, twenty to twenty-five miles away by road, they heard about

His furious activity at Capernaum and "went out" or set out to constrain Him. They arrived on the scene at verse 31, after His contest with the Scribes and Pharisees. Jesus' relatives sought to take custody of Him by force because they felt He was "out of his mind," in a state of excitement bordering on insanity. Maclear observed, "They deemed the zeal and daily devotion to His labour of love a sort of ecstasy or religious enthusiasm, which made Him no longer master of Himself" (p. 76).

While the relatives of Jesus had one theory to explain His reckless devotion to mission, the scribes and Pharisees from the hostile party in Jerusalem had a less kindly explanation. They charged (imperfect tense, "repeatedly charged") that He was energized by Beelzebub (origin uncertain but clearly referring to the devil), the prince of demons, to cast out demons. The accusation is actually double: that He was personally empowered by Satan or in league with him, and that by satanic power He cast out demons. Evidently they were spreading these charges behind Jesus' back because in verse 23 He "called them" to Him, formally summoned them. Then He proceeded to confront them before the crowd with the question: "How can Satan cast out Satan?" He does not say, "How can Satan cast out demons?" but identifies the demons with their ruler, for they are one, and shows the absurdity of their claim on the face of it.

Following His clear question, Jesus introduces two parabolic statements. If neither a kingdom nor a household could stand when divided against itself, the same would be true of the empire of Satan. "Is coming to an end" refers not to the existence of Satan but his rule over his kingdom. "But" (a strong adversative, v. 27), by a strongly contrasting figure He shows the true state of the case. It is impossible to break into a brigand's ("strong man's") house and seize the plunder he has stashed away there, unless one first overpowers the brigand; then it is possible to plunder his house. The meaning is clear. Jesus, not in league with Satan, has overpowered him. And having done so, He may then take (free) His "goods," unfortunate human beings Satan controls through his demonic subordinates. In casting out demons from possessed individuals He shows that He was not in league with Satan but had defeated him, that He had become the master of the master of the demons.

In verses 28-30, Jesus turns from calm reasoning to solemn warning. The Scribes and Pharisees are not merely mistaken theorists but are in a dangerous moral condition. "All sins shall be forgiven," a comprehensive view of divine grace; all kinds and classes of sins shall be

forgiven, even "blasphemy" (malicious misrepresentation derogatory of
God's honor and power). But there is an "eternal sin" (rendering of the
best Greek text), one eternal in guilt, for which one "never has forgiveness." This sin blasphemes or maliciously misrepresents the Holy Spirit
and is incurred "because they kept on saying, He has an unclean spirit."
In hardness of heart they deliberately attributed to satanic enablement
Jesus' power to do miracles, which were actually done in the power of
the Holy Spirit. This sin is not so much an act as a state of sin; note the
continuation of action in verse 30, "kept on saying." No doubt if any of
these enemies of Jesus had reversed their attitude toward Jesus they
could have been forgiven. But this state of sin if persevered in would
exclude one from pardon. "Is guilty" literally is entangled in or held fast
by guilt so that he cannot escape.

New relatives (3:31-35). "And his mother and his brothers arrived."
"While he was still talking to the people" (Matt. 12:46), after the
confrontation over the unpardonable sin, Jesus' mother and brothers
arrived from Nazareth. The usual conclusion is that Joseph was no
longer living at the time and that these were younger sons of Mary and
Joseph, born after Jesus. Those who seek to preserve the perpetual
virginity of Mary argue that they were sons of Joseph by a previous
marriage or that they were cousins of Jesus (cf. Mark 6:3). The family
members arrived from Nazareth, apparently to take Jesus away from His
ministry for rest and recuperation (cf. 3:21). Perhaps they also had
learned that the Pharisees and Herodians had plotted against His life
and wondered if He should reduce His activity so as not to antagonize
them so much.

"Standing outside," outside the house or the crowd surrounding
Jesus, "they sent to him, calling him." Either they sent in a messenger to
tell Him they were there and asked Him to come out to talk with them,
or they passed along their request through the crowd by word of mouth.
The latter seems to have been the case; "and they say to him" implies
that some on the edge of the crowd got His attention and delivered the
message. "The crowd was sitting in a circle around him," evidently
cross-legged on the floor or on the ground.

And He said, "Who are my mother and my brothers?" As A. B.
Bruce commented, ". . . an apparently harsh question, but He knew
what they had come for" (p. 363). He had no more intention of allow-
ing His relatives to stop His ministry than to allow His religious opponents to do so. Then as His eye swept the whole circle of His audience

(cf. 3:5, but with no look of anger), He stretched out His hand toward His disciples (Matt. 12:49) and said, "Here are my mother and my brothers." Since the disciples were all men, evidently He was speaking of something higher than blood ties. But it should not be thought that Jesus was repudiating His family. He demonstrated His tender concern for His mother even during the agony of crucifixion (John 19:26,27), and His brothers James and Jude later became significant in the Christian movement. In His next statement Jesus made His point more specific, "Whoever does the will of God, this one is my brother and sister and mother" (v. 35). Father is evidently omitted because Christ reserved reference to a father to the heavenly Father. Henceforth all who hear and believe and follow God's Son are viewed as belonging to the family of God. Whether or not Jesus' relatives ever managed to talk with Him on this occasion is left open to question.

For Further Study

A Review of Mark 1 – 3

1. Make five observations on Jesus' method and spirit in His miracles.

2. State five important things learned by the Twelve in these chapters.

3. State seven important claims made by Jesus.

4. State five objections to Jesus from His enemies.

Chapter 6

A Day of Kingdom Parables
(Mark 4:1-41)

This chapter seems to mark a departure from the usual emphasis on action in this Gospel. Yet, it should be noted that Jesus uttered these parables on the same day as all the action of Mark 3:20-35. Matthew 13:1 clearly states it was the "same day." Moreover, at the end of the day, after teaching was over, the tempestuous movement of 4:35-41 occurred.

The sower (4:1-20). Jesus went out by the shore of the Sea of Galilee to teach, and large crowds so mobbed Him that He got into a boat and sat on its deck to teach them. Whether the Twelve were in the boat or on land is not clear. The Greek indicates a vessel of fair size which could not be brought right onto shore. "He continued to teach them many things in parables"—short fictitious narratives with a moral or spiritual application. As Jesus taught, no doubt many of the things He talked about were visible to Him and His hearers—grain fields, mustard trees, thorns, stony ground, and much more. On this occasion the Master used parables to convey truth concerning various aspects of the kingdom.

A sower "went forth" to sow. He went out from his house and garden plot into open country to carry on work familiar to all peasants of Galilee. The scattering of seed on the fields was the standard form of sowing seed until the Englishman Jethro Tull invented the seed drill for sowing seed about 1701. Some seed fell along the edge of the field on a hard footpath or road, and it lay exposed on the surface where birds could eat it. Other seed fell on rocky soil, not rocks mixed into the soil but rock covered with a thin layer of soil. The sun beat down on the rock, causing rapid germination. Subsequently the sun scorched and withered the plants which found themselves in dried soil and could not send

39

their roots deeper to tap moisture. Yet other seed fell among thorns, evidently in parts of the field where roots of thornbushes had not been plowed up, and where seeds of thorns were in the soil. Soon thorns sprouted and grew faster than the wheat, stifling it and preventing it from bearing. Most of the field consisted of good soil and most of the seed landed on good soil, where it had varying degrees of yield according to the fertility of the soil. It is important to recognize that the seed was of equally good quality; problems of germination and fruit bearing lay in the soil. "Who hath ears to hear, let him hear." This was not just a nice story; it had significant truth to communicate.

"When he was done." Some time later in the day, when the crowd had dispersed and Jesus was accompanied by only the Twelve and another group of dedicated disciples, they asked Him what this parable meant. Mark interrupts the recital of the parables at this point so the interpretation of the sower parable may appear next to the parable itself.

"To you is given the mystery [secret] of the kingom of God." To you, insiders or initiates, like the initiates of the Greco-Roman mystery religions, is given the privilege of understanding—in this case the secret of God's kingdom. The mystery lies not in the fact that it is "mysterious" or "strange" or "difficult" to interpret, but rather that true meaning cannot be known until revealed. Also, mystery in the New Testament refers to something not previously known by men but now imparted by divine revelation to those qualified to receive it. So parables were used to teach initiates without revealing information to "those outside our circle." They are a condemnation on the wilfully hostile.

Verse 12 sometimes has been treated as inconsistent with the love of God and His desire that all should come to repentance. But it should be noted that Jesus had been very direct with His enemies up to that point; note, for instance, Mark 3:1-6. The Scribes and Pharisees knew full well that what was expected of them was acceptance of Jesus' messiahship. If they had done so at any time, they could have become part of the inner circle, the initiate, and could have learned the most intimate truths of Christ thereafter. What is hidden in these parables is not truth necessary for salvation, but information on God's workings on earth. In fact, throughout the New Testament the truth about how one may become a Christian—by faith in the finished work of Christ on the cross—is clear as a bell to all who will read. Not so clear to the non-Christian are such things as the meaning of some of the theology of Romans or Hebrews or the prophecy of Revelation. God has never hidden from people what they need to know to gain salvation.

Jesus now proceeds to interpret the sower parable as an example of interpretation in dealing with other parables. The sower is not identified, but he evidently represents Christ or others who preach the Gospel. The seed stands for the word of God. And the four soils represent four attitudes toward the word on the part of hearers. In the case of the first type of soil, the birds represent Satan (here as elsewhere in the book treated as a real personality), who comes and snatches away the seed before it has a chance to germinate. ". . . the hardened hearts of the hearers do not give the Word a chance to penetrate below the surface of their thoughts" (Hiebert, p. 103).

Thin soil above a rock substratum represents individuals who "with joy," with enthusiasm or emotional fervor, "are temporary" adherents to the truth. But it never permeates beyond a superficial level in their lives; it never makes a fundamental change. When the heat of trials descends they just wilt away. Seed sown among thorns does germinate and sends down its roots, but the plant is so choked by impediments to growth that it bears no fruit. The impediments are described as distracting anxieties of the age that cut a man to pieces, the deceptive nature of wealth which promises to satisfy and never does, and the craving or passionate desire for other things. The good soil represents those persons who continue to hear the word, continue to accept it, and continue to bear fruit. The three present participles in the Greek of verse 20 indicate durative action. "These are people who hear, who understand, who are sincere, and who appropriate the message of the Gospel permanently" (Burdick, p. 996). This parable describes the various responses to Christ's message as He preached it and responses to the gospel during this present age as the message of Christ is preached. It is important to note that most hearers did not receive the truth, even when Christ proclaimed it. Modern servants of Christ should not conclude that if they enjoyed greater power of the Holy Spirit they would necessarily sweep the masses into the kingdom. But of course such an observation should not be used as an excuse for laxness or low expectation of success in the work of God.

Lamp and measure (4:21-25). The message of these verses evidently is the stewardship of truth. Members of the kingdom who have received spiritual insight or light have the responsibility to spread that light. Especially here Jesus refers to the responsibility of the disciples. A "lamp" was the small clay lamp that burned olive oil and normally could be held in the palm of one's hand. The "bushel" or "measure" was about the size of our peck measure. If put under such a measure, light not only would be hid but in time would go out for lack of air. The "bed" could be a bed for sleeping (commonly a bedroll under which one could not put anything) or more likely a dining couch on which one would recline while eating. The individual supported himself on his left arm while eating with the right hand. A "lampstand" normally would be a projection from a wall or a niche in it; in wealthier homes it might be a separate stand. "A lamp is not brought in to be put under a measure or a bed, is it?" In the nature of the case a lamp is used to disseminate light.

Translations generally obscure the real intent of verse 22. A proper rendering would be, "Nothing is hidden, except in order that it might be made known." Items of value—jewelry, expensive tableware, and the like—have no value if never used or displayed. They are kept concealed for use at the right time. Just so, certain aspects of divine truth may be reserved for the disciples for a while, but after the Ascension they were to become general knowledge. Periodically in the Gospels truths deliberately are to be held back temporarily, e.g., Mark 9:9. Verse 23 is an appeal to try to understand the parable.

Of course verses 24-25 have nothing to do with acquisition and distribution of material goods; the subject is spiritual truth. Beck provides a helpful translation of verse 24: "'Be careful what you hear!' He told them. 'The measure you measure with will be used for you. Yes, you will get even more.'" Here is an appeal for spiritual perception. Hiebert puts the matter succinctly: "Truth received and carefully assimilated enlarges one's capacity to receive more truth. . . . The man who does not use his ability to understand the truth thereby blunts his ability to understand it. Disuse of spiritual ability results in spiritual atrophy" (p. 108). The effective use of the mind sharpens the mind.

Commentators generally seem to stop with the understanding of truth in their treatment of verses 24-25. It seems, however, that these two verses relate directly to what Jesus was saying in verses 21-23. In other words, verses 21-25 put together teach that the follower of Jesus has the responsibility to disseminate the truth; as one does so he will get a better grasp on the truth himself. If he fails to unfold the truth to others, his own ability to understand it will seem to shrivel. How often those of us who train teachers have heard our charges say, "I never really understood that until I had to explain it to someone else," or "When I began to teach I really started to learn," or "When I give out to others, knowledge [or the truth] becomes so much more exciting to me."

Seedtime to harvest (4:26-29). This parable, appearing in Mark only, picks up where the parable of the sower leaves off. Here there is comment on the seed which has been sown in good soil growing secretly. Though the second parable makes it clear that followers of Jesus have a certain responsibility to disseminate the truth, it is easy for them to exaggerate their importance and they are prone to discouragement if they do not see immediate results. This parable shows that the actual growth process in the spiritual world occurs apart from our interference and that maturation takes a normal amount of time; we must exercise patience until it is finished. The sower sows the seed and then will sleep and rise many times while the seed sprouts and grows. He is ignorant of the process but nature's secret processes continue to operate anyway. Just so there is a mysterious growth of the kingdom in the heart and life. "The earth produces of itself," *automatically* (Greek); this is so because the seed, the word, "contains life which, when placed in the proper environment, produces growth. . . . the message of the Gospel, by its very nature, when sown in men's hearts produces growth and fruitfulness spontaneously" (Burdick, p. 996).

"But whenever the crop permits, he immediately sends forth the sickle, because the harvest stands ready" (v. 29). After the seed has been going through the maturation process long enough harvest time comes; after the word of truth has been maturing long enough, it leads a person to the point of being a true child of the kingdom. "He sends forth the sickle" is the same construction that appears in John 4:38. The sickle stands for the reapers who use it. Just as in the natural world there is a long process involved in a seed's growing up and bearing fruit, so in the spiritual world a lapse of time and much effort may be required between the time the seed of the gospel is sown and it bears fruit in a full profession of faith. The sickle is not exercised in judgment, but in gathering the ripened grain which is now ready to be brought into the Master's storehouse (kingdom).

The mustard seed (4:30-32). The previous parable described internal growth and manner of growth of the kingdom; this one depicts external growth and extent of growth. The kingdom of God is compared to the mustard seed, one of the smallest of all seeds. Palestinian mustard is a tiny black seed like that of the petunia. It produces a very large shrub, often over ten to twelve feet in height. One gets no help in understanding this passage of Scripture from visualizing North American mustard, which grows as a low bush and produces large yellow seeds. The kingdom, like a mustard seed, started small. Its insignificant beginnings would not lead one to expect anything large, but such was not the case. It was destined to make a tremendous impact in the world. The main point of the parable is clear. Some would add a word about the birds, however. If birds represent Satan in the first parable, they may do so here. If this is the case, possibly they indicate a mixture of good and evil in the great tree of Christendom.

Spoke only parables (4:33-34). "Many such parables." Mark knew of other parables spoken on that day besides the ones he recorded in his Gospel. It is clear from all the Gospels that many additional parables, miracles, and teachings of Christ were known; but each writer chose what suited his purpose, under the direction of the Holy Spirit. "Able to hear" refers to the capacity of Jesus' audience to comprehend His teachings. Since He addressed the crowd only in parables, the indication is that generally they were unprepared to understand or accept Him or the kingdom. "Privately to his own disciples he was explaining everything." "His own disciples" intimates unique personal relationship to them. "He explained," He interpreted knotty points or riddles or solved problems of understanding.

Peace be still (4:35-41). "That same day, when it was evening." What a day it had been! Starting with a contest with scribes and Pharisees and continuing with a visit from His mother and brothers and hours of teaching the crowds and His disciples, it was now to end with some relief from the pressure by a sail across the Sea of Galilee. Their destination on "the other side" was not far away, probably not more than seven or eight miles, and was clearly visible from Capernaum. But it was a region where He was not known. Though Jesus initiated the journey, which occurred around sundown, the disciples carried out the arrangements: "they take him." Conceivably the company sailed in a fishing boat that belonged to the partnership of Peter, Andrew, James, and John. Again Peter's vivid eyewitness recollections add a detail: "other boats were with him." No doubt these were filled with followers or people from the crowd who wanted to hear Him further.

Suddenly a great storm arose. This was not an uncommon phenomenon because the lake is about 700 feet below sea level and high winds frequently sweep down on the water through ravines in the hills surrounding the lake. Soon the "waves were beating in the boat" and the "boat was in the process of filling." Meanwhile Jesus had gone to the stern of the boat and had fallen asleep "on the cushion," probably the steersman's leather cushion. Even though the wind was blowing violently, the waves were spraying water all around Him, and the ship was pitching violently, the exhausted Master was asleep. Finally the impatient disciples awakened Him: "Teacher, is it of no concern to you that we are perishing?" "Thoroughly aroused, he rebuked the wind, and said to the sea, 'Peace! Be Still!'" or "be muzzled." Wuest translates, "Be getting calm; hush up and stay that way" (p. 98). "The wind stopped suddenly and there was a great calm." This evidently was a miracle. Winds sometimes do stop blowing but they leave waters choppy for a while; in this case not only did the wind stop blowing but the water became as glass.

Having spoken to the elements, the Master turned to the disciples and asked two questions: "Why are you afraid?" Why do you have such cowardly fear? "Have you no faith yet?" Hiebert observes, "The second question . . . pointed to the fact that they had not yet apprehended the true significance of the fact that the kingdom was present in the Person and work of Jesus" (p. 116). Evidently they did have some faith or they would not have awakened Jesus. The way they upbraided Him for sleeping indicates that they thought He might do something about their predicament if He were awake. Mark does not say that the disciples responded to Jesus, but they did converse among themselves. The topic of conversation is summed up in Mark's question: "Who then is this, that even the wind and the sea obey Him?" (NASB). Exorcism of demons had been done by others. Miracles of healing had occurred in history; for instance, the prophets Elijah and Elisha had performed miracles. But it was quite another matter for a great religious leader to command the forces of nature.

For Further Study

1. Evaluate the method of teaching by parables. Why and when did Jesus use this method?

2. Explain Mark 4:12. Compare Isaiah 6:6-10; John 12:37-40; Acts 28:24-28.

3. What is the place of Mark 4:35-41 in the chapter. Project yourself into this incident. What do you feel? hear? see?

4. Does this chapter answer any problems in the life of today?

Chapter 7

Faith Failing and Triumphant
(Mark 5:1-43)

Chapter 5 is a series of miracles performed on the eastern and western sides of the Sea of Galilee. Faith is demonstrated by the demon-possessed man, Jairus, and the woman with the issue of blood. Lack of faith appears in the Gerasene request that Jesus leave the region and the conclusion of members of Jairus's household that Jesus could do nothing after Jairus's daughter had died. All of these miracles bear witness to the great power, if not the deity, of Christ because each reflects an impossible situation: the uncontrollable Gerasene demoniac, a woman with an issue of blood who had been going to doctors for years without success, the dead daughter of Jairus.

The Gerasene demoniac (5:1-20). "They came to the other side of the sea." Jesus and His disciples arrived together, but the disciples are conspicuously silent in the first half of this chapter. They are evidently observers in the first five chapters of the book; in chapter 6 they will become apprentices. "Gerasenes" is apparently the correct reading; probably the town referred to was located about midway along the eastern shore of the Sea of Galilee and may have been at the site now called Kersa. "A man" met Jesus; Luke likewise speaks of one (8:27) but Matthew mentions two (8:28). Presumably the one was so much fiercer than the others that Mark and Luke do not even take note of the second. If indeed it was customary for him to make the way impassable for travelers (Matt. 8:28), then it would be natural for him to accost Jesus and the disciples. This fearsome individual made his habitual dwelling in the tombs (probably caves) and had demonic strength which prevented keeping him bound for long. As they were able, the townspeople bound him hand and foot, but he wrenched apart the chains on

46

his hands and by constant friction "rubbed through" the fetters (probably of cord or wood) on his feet. Night and day he continually (without long intervals), restlessly moved about in the tombs and on the mountains uttering inarticulate shrieks or screams and slashing himself with stones.

As the demon-possessed man saw Jesus from a distance, he ran toward Him, apparently not with the intent of threatening Him as he had other travelers. "Crying out with a loud voice" (v. 7), he screamed or shrieked his demonic yell before entering into articulate conversation. "What have I to do with you" might be rendered "What do we have in common?" Here as on previous occasions in the book the demon recognizes Jesus for who He is, but in this case he addresses Him as "Son of the most High God." This not only attests Jesus' identity with the Father but also distinguishes the Father as above all other gods. When the parallel accounts of Matthew and Luke are placed alongside that of Mark, it is clear that the demon is worried about being thrown into the abyss (Luke 8:31) in torment before the final day of judgment (Matt. 8:29). So the demons not only recognize Jesus for who He is but they are aware of their ultimate destiny and have at least a vague idea of when the judgment will come in relation to other events in history. In Mark the demon even uses the formula of exorcism to persuade Jesus not to send him into the abyss: "I adjure you by God."

This is a most unusual text on demon possession in many ways, not the least of which is the apparent fact that the demon does not come out of the demon-possessed man when Jesus first tells him to do so (v. 8). The demon seeks to parley with Jesus about its future. Then Jesus asks the demon for its name, which has been construed as a means of demonstrating to all the onlookers that Jesus was dealing with a host of demons. On at least two other occasions individuals were indwelt by multiple demons: Mary Magdalene with seven (Mark 16:9; Luke 8:2), and an unknown man with seven (Matt. 12:43; Luke 11:24). The demon replies, "Legion: for we are many." The legion was the name of the chief division of the Roman army. At full strength it was 6,000, but it usually was not fully manned. Reference is at least to thousands, and perhaps the use of this particular name also symbolized great power and terror to enemies. Then the demon begged not to be sent "out of the country." The point is not that they had some special attachment to this locale or that demons are assigned to various parts of the world. When Mark 5:10 is compared with the parallel statement in Luke 8:31, it is clear that the demons were concerned about being sent out of the country "into the abyss" before their time.

The presence of a large herd of swine in the vicinity indicates Jewish laxness in observing the law. This was, after all, Jewish territory under the control of Herod Philip; and there is no mention in the narrative about Jesus' ministry to Gentiles, as is customarily the case on those rare occasions when He met their needs (e.g., Luke 7:1-10; Mark 7:24-30). Why demons should want to go into swine is difficult to discover. They could hardly appeal to enter another human being and presumably did not want to be disembodied. Lenski makes the suggestion, ". . . that according to the law which God gave the Jews swine were unclean, and these spirits were also morally and spiritually unclean and were thus in affinity with the unclean swine" (p. 211). Possibly, too, this was all part of the demonic plan to hinder Jesus' ministry. Satan may have put it into the minds of his henchmen to enter the swine, to destroy them, and thus to hinder the reception of Jesus' ministry in the region. The truth is, no one really knows why the demons wanted to enter the swine. Lenski's conclusion is as astute as any, ". . . devilish actions are always more or less irrational . . . and are thus beyond the domain of proper reason" (p. 211).

At any rate, Jesus permitted the demons their request. If the owners were Jews, He merely permitted judgment on their breaking of the law. If they were Gentiles a moral problem is created for which there is no easy answer. Many try to solve the difficulty by noting that the demons, not Jesus, made the request to enter the swine; and they were responsible for their destruction. All three accounts of this event record that the demons actually entered the swine and caused them to rush into the water and be drowned; only Mark indicates that the number was 2,000. Perhaps Peter knew this from talking to the swineherds; possibly the disciples made their own estimate.

"The herdsmen fled," no doubt because of their fear of such overwhelming power, and also because of fear of what might happen to them for any dereliction of duty. They would have to defend themselves before their employers as soon as possible to shift the blame from their shoulders. Their account of the miracle brought many to see the phenomenon. The contrast in the appearance and conduct of the demoniac was overwhelming: "sitting" instead of roving restlessly; "clothed" instead of naked; "in his right mind," sane and self-controlled, instead of characterized by frenzied insanity; "who had had the legion," no longer under the control of demons. The onlookers were "seized with fear" in the face of such divine power and apparently shrank from Jesus with apprehension of what else He might do.

Although the herdsmen had filled the countryside with an account of what had happened, the crowd now got a report of the event on location (v. 16). Possibly even the disciples chimed in with some of the details, though they are not mentioned. "Then they began to beg Jesus to depart." Apparently some started the request and others joined in until the whole crowd was urging Him to leave (Luke 8:37 indicates they were unanimous in their desire). Probably they feared further financial losses if Jesus remained. There is no hint of rejoicing over the rehabilitation of the demoniac nor any desire for healing from various diseases as in Galilee. Lenski concludes that the failure of the owners to censure Jesus for destruction of the swine is an indication they were Jews. As Jews they would have found it embarrassing even to admit ownership of swine. Gentiles would have raised a ruckus over destruction of property (p. 215).

Jesus did not force Himself on people. He left rather promptly with His disciples, failing to find in this secluded spot the rest and refreshment He had sought. We are left to wonder what happened to the demons who had drowned the swine. The restored demoniac was refused permission to accompany the apostolic band. Jesus did not need any more witnesses of healing or expulsion of demons in Galilee; many were already there. This man could herald the good news about Jesus in an area otherwise uninformed about Him or hostile to Him. Instead of a command to be quiet as had been customary in cases of Galilean miracle working, Jesus took the limitations off this man. He was to be a witness in an area otherwise without one (v. 19). The convert was faithful and gave his testimony throughout "Decapolis." Decapolis means *ten cities* and was a league of Greco-Roman towns mostly east of the Jordan River. Hellenistic and Roman rulers of the area built up these cities to maintain their control of the area and to counter Jewish nationalism and religious exclusivism.

Jairus's request (5:21-24). It is clear from Matthew 9:1 that as Jesus and His disciples recrossed the Sea of Galilee after restoring the Gerasene demoniac they returned to Capernaum. It is clear, too, that the miracles of Mark 4:35 - 5:43 are topically rather than chronologically arranged. The events of Mark 5:1-20 actually occurred before the healing of the paralytic in Mark 2 and the subsequent call of Levi and the feast at his house. Apparently after Levi's feast a great crowd gathered around Jesus by the seashore. While Jesus was talking to them, Jairus, one of the rulers of the synagogue, came to Him. This important man, one of those in charge of the services and property of the synagogue, fell down prostrate at Jesus' feet. This was more than oriental obeisance. His only daughter, about twelve years of age (Luke 8:42) lay "at the point of death" (Mark 5:23). He "kept begging" "come and lay your hands on her" (RSV). Jairus had great faith but apparently felt the Master had to be present in person to heal; at least He always had been as far as Jairus knew. No verbal response of Jesus is recorded. He simply started to go to Jairus's house. The curious, inconsiderate crowd, sensing an opportunity to see another miracle, "thronged him," pressed Him on all sides, and greatly impeded His movements toward the sick child when every moment was crucial.

Woman with issue of blood (5:25-34). In the crowd was a woman who had had a chronic issue of blood for twelve years. This is thought to have been a uterine issue, which was not only painful but also resulted in social ostracism (Lev. 15:19-27). All those twelve years she had been going from doctor to doctor trying all their good suggestions and the quack remedies of an infant science, until finally she had spent all her assets and was actually worse off than before. Luke, a doctor, was not as hard on the medical profession as Mark (see Luke 8:43).

Finally, in her extremity, the woman decided to go to Jesus. She gradually pushed her way through the crowd until she was able to touch Him from behind. But she did not want to attract His attention so she merely touched lightly the hem or fringe of His outer garment (Matt. 9:20; Luke 8:44). She "kept saying" to herself that if she could only touch His garments she would be healed. Presumably she was too embarrassed to come to Jesus and explain her malady before a crowd, so she took this course of action.

"And immediately the inner source of her bleeding was dried up," and she was conscious that the healing was complete and she had been delivered of her scourge. Immediately also Jesus recognized "that power had gone forth from him." The magnetic touch of faith had called forth from the Master a flow of healing power; He knew her condition and had honored her faith. He turned around and asked, "Who touched my garments?" The disciples, with Peter as spokesman (Luke 8:45), pointed out that the question was rather foolish because the crowd had been pressing Him on every side. But He kept repeating the question (imperfect tense in Greek) "and he kept looking all around." His eyes wandered from one face to another, searching out the person responsible. The miracle had to be revealed for the sake of the woman, to solidify her faith, and to eliminate any superstitious ideas about the method of healing (e.g., that His clothing had any miraculous power); for the sake of the multitude—to lead some to faith; and for the sake of the King and His kingdom—miracles not only led to faith but they accredited the man and His message.

Evidently Jesus' eyes finally rested on the woman and she knew she would have to confess (Luke 8:47). She came in "fear" (inner condition) and "trembling" (outward evidence of fear) and told the whole embarrassing story. No doubt it is from this confession that details of verses 25-29 were learned. Her fear probably was caused by the embarrassment of telling her story before the crowd and her uncertainty of what Jesus would say or do. Comentators frequently note that she may have feard His anger because, according to the law, touching one afflicted as she was would have made Him ceremonially unclean until evening (Lev. 15:19). His treatement was gracious: "Daughter" speaks of His loving concern and He is not recorded to have addressed anyone else by this title. "Your faith has saved you," has healed you from your physical affliction. "Go in peace," go in the assurance of future peace, "and be well from your plague," continue to have sound health.

Raising Jairus's daughter (5:35-43). While this whole episode was in progress, Jairus must have been increasingly impatient, shifting on one foot and then the other, fully conscious that the life of his dear daughter was ebbing and almost gone. Speed was of the essence. "While he [Jesus] was still speaking," pronouncing His blessing on the healed woman, messengers arrived from Jairus's home with word that his daughter was dead and added, "Why trouble the Teacher further?" While they may have had a certain amount of faith in Jesus' ability to heal, evidently they did not think He had the power to raise anyone from the dead. How much faith Jairus had is not clear. However little it may have been, Jesus was determined to bolster it. Disregarding what was being said, Jesus said to Jairus, "Fear not, only continue to believe" (v. 36). Do not be overcome by the fear that there is no hope for your daughter but continue to have faith I can do something. Then He finally dismissed the curious crowd and took only Peter, James, and John along with Jairus to the ruler's house. Here begins that special tutelage of this inner circle who were to accompany Jesus on other significant occasions (the Transfiguration, Mark 9:2; agony in the Garden, 14:33). Hiebert sees the presence of three disciples here as three legal witnesses to events about to occur (Deut. 17:6) (p. 133).

When the company came to Jairus's house the professional mourners were making a terrible din. When a death took place, the female members of a family and professional mourning women would utter a shrill and piercing cry which announced the death to the neighborhood. Thereafter mourners would wail and flutists would make a loud lamentation. This was not only a Jewish practice (see 2 Chron. 35:25; Jer. 9:17,18) but was carried on generally in the Near East. They were demonstrating not only outside but inside the house as well. To those inside He said, "Why are you making such an uproar? The child did not die but is sleeping." Jesus' statement has led to two interpretations: (1) that the girl was only in a coma and was apparently dead; (2) that she was actually dead. The first view builds on a literal acceptance of Jesus' words. The second, which certainly must be correct, holds that Jesus was speaking figuratively of a condition that was temporary and that she would awaken soon. According to Luke, the mourners knew she was dead (Luke 8:53). Jesus used the same terminology when referring to the death of Lazarus (John 11:11-14).

The mourners laughed in Jesus' face, but He put them all out of the house and took the parents and the disciples into the child's room. Then grasping her by the hand as one would the hand of the living, He evidently raised her up a little and simultaneously commanded "Talitha cumi," the Aramaic for "Little girl, arise." "Immediately the girl stood up [point action] and started to walk" (continued action). Since she was twelve she was old enough to do so. Luke adds that "her spirit came again" (8:55), supporting the view that she had actually died.

"They were overcome with amazement" (RSV) is a fair English representation of the reaction to this miracle. Actually the Greek is hard to translate, combining ideas of amazement coupled with fear, ecstasy, and being removed out of one's senses. These disciples had now seen Jesus as victor over demons, all kinds of sickness, the forces of nature, and death. The command in verse 43 that "no one should know this" evidently refers to unnecessary publicity on the part of the parents. Certainly all sorts of persons would know about her recovery as she carried on normal activity. Then, lest the parents should in their excitement forget to feed this girl who had so long been without food, He adds a reminder that reflects His tender thoughtfulness.

For Further Study

Review of Chapters 1 - 5

1. List the miracles in the book thus far. What aspects is Mark apparently trying to emphasize?

2. What characters have been introduced and why?

3. What forces of opposition are introduced and why?

4. In what way are the disciples introduced? What lessons have they learned?

5. What teachings have been introduced and why?

Chapter 8

Beginning of Discipleship
(Mark 6:1-56)

Up to this point the disciples have been observers of events, generally silent bystanders, while Jesus and others have initiated action. Now they will become participants in the action as they are commissioned to their ministry in a new sense, as they perform tasks under Jesus' direction, and as they count the cost of discipleship while meditating on the murder of John the Baptist.

Nazareth rejection (6:1-6). Jesus left Capernaum "and came to his own country," Nazareth and its environs; "and his disciples follow him." This visit is certainly recorded by Matthew (13:53-58). Some think Luke 4:16-31 is a parallel account, but several considerations indicate that it concerned the earlier rejection at Nazareth. As Matthew makes clear (Matt. 4:13; 13:53-58) there were two rejections at Nazareth: one at the beginning of our Lord's Galilean ministry, which resulted in removal to Capernaum; the other at the height of His Galilean ministry after teaching the great kingdom parables (sower, etc.). He called the disciples after the first rejection; now He returns with them ("his disciples follow him"). All the group is together again after the inner circle of Peter, James, and John had been separated from the rest for the raising of Jairus' daughter.

"The sabbath having come, he began to teach." Apparently He did not begin to do any teaching in town before the Sabbath and evidently there was no crowd that had gathered around Him for healing. Many hearers were "astonished" at Jesus' performance; "flabbergasted" is a truer representation of the Greek. "Where did this man get these things?" (NASB). "This man" is derogatory in contrast to "these things," which are amazing. "What is the wisdom given to him?" Astounded at

His wisdom, they cannot conceive of it as being His by nature but assume it has been imparted to Him. Nor could they account for His miracles, not wrought in Nazareth but constantly reported from various places in Galilee. After all, He had not worked miracles in His earlier years there, nor had any other members of His family.

Verse 3 gives specific reasons for their wonder. He was a "carpenter" (v. 3), mentioned only here in the New Testament, making furniture, house fittings, and utensils. Actual house building in Palestine was almost exclusively done in stone. "Son of Mary" is highly unusual because a man normally was spoken of as the son of his father, even when the father was dead. Some expositors take this to be an inference of His illegitimate birth. His brothers were known and named: James, Joses, Judas, and Simon. James later was destined to lead the church in Jerusalem and to write the Epistle of James; Judas (Jude) wrote the Epistle of Jude. "Sisters here with us" probably indicates that they were married and lived in or near Nazareth. "They took offense," they found occasion of stumbling in Him; they saw in Him what hindered them from accepting His authority. "They could not explain Him, so they rejected Him" (Wuest, p. 121). Jesus responded with a proverbial statement: "A prophet is not without honor except in his home town and among his own relatives and in his own household" (NASB). Jesus' observation involves a claim to the prophetic office and shows clearly the main function of a prophet—that of proclaiming rather than predicting truth. Jesus evidently had not been predicting the future and rarely would do so later on.

"He could do no mighty work" does not mean He was actually incapable of doing any but that in His manner of functioning He chose only to expend Himself on behalf of those who responded in faith. Perhaps this provides an answer to a question sometimes raised in a community. Often when a problem or need arises or a tragedy occurs, non-Christians or peripherally Christian people will say, "Why doesn't God do something about this?" (as if God in His benevolence is bound to do great things for all people all the time). One is tempted to ask such persons another question in response, "Have you asked Him to do something?" (See James 4:2.) Jesus healed only a few sickly individuals who came to Him, and then left town; there is no evidence He ever returned. They had had a second chance and had rejected Him again. He does not indefinitely offer Himself to those who will have nothing to do with Him. Leaving Nazareth, "He went round about the villages in a circle"; this probably means He preached in the villages in the adjacent country encircling Nazareth.

Commission of the Twelve (6:7-13). Apparently Jesus felt that the disciples had had sufficient observation; now they could try their wings, so to speak. And His own efforts could be multiplied. He sent them out "two by two" so they could help and encourage each other, so they would supplement each other's message, and so their hearers would be more impressed by a double witness. As Wuest observes, the verb translated "to send" is "to send forth as an ambassador on a commission to represent one and to perform some task" (p. 122). Jesus' address on this occasion is reported in greater detail in Matthew 10 where a list of pairs is given (perhaps as they were sent on this occasion) and where indications of a larger mission to the world appear. "He kept on giving them [throughout the tour] authority [delegated authority] over unclean spirits." Then follows a summary of the Master's charge. Take nothing for the road except a walking stick, no food, no traveler's bag, no money in the folds of their belt, but they were to provide themselves with sandals (in case they were presently barefooted) and they were not to take along extra clothing. They were to go in absolute dependence on God.

As they engage in their ministry, they will be invited to accept lodging. When they accept an offer they are to stay in that house as long as they are in the village and are not to shop around for something better. If a village (or possibly a house) refuses to hear their message, they are to engage in a ceremonial act of shaking the dirt of that place from their sandals as a warning of the consequences of rejecting the message of the kingdom. So they went out and preached a message of repentance and "continued to cast out demons," apparently on numerous instances, and continued to heal many who were sick. Their destination must have been some of the towns of Galilee and the duration of their ministry is uncertain, perhaps a few weeks. Meanwhile Jesus engaged in a ministry of His own (Matt. 11:1). One should be careful of adopting Jesus' instructions in this passage as a way of life for Christian workers. When this brief Galilean evangelistic tour was over, the disciples returned to their previous way of life. Even the apostle Paul on his missionary journeys commonly supported himself by His own labor or by offerings from churches, and apparently carried a few belongings with him. The commands of Christ on this occasion must have been a temporary expedient.

Murder of John the Baptist (6:14-29). The reputation of Jesus now came to the attention of government officials. "King Herod," not Herod the Great but Herod Antipas, ruler of Galilee and Perea (territory east of the Jordan between the Sea of Galilee and the Dead Sea), had learned of Jesus' ministry. "He said" is probably the preferred reading of the Greek. Herod heard of Jesus' ministry and concluded that John the Baptist had risen from the dead (even though his Hellenistic religion denied the Resurrection) and "that is why these powers are working in him" (v. 14). Vincent explains, "He knew that John wrought no miracles when alive, but he thought that death had put him into connection with the unseen world, and enabled him to wield its powers" (p. 192). As others tried to explain the ministry of Jesus, they "said," repeatedly said (it was frequently asserted) that He was Elijah—an understandable assertion because of the expectation that the return of Elijah would precede the coming of Messiah (Mal. 4:5). Others merely considered Him to be one of the prophets. "But whenever Herod heard." Herod was so conscience smitten over his murder of John the Baptist that the guilt of it was constantly on his mind; and whenever news of Jesus' doings came to him, he just knew that John had come back from the dead.

The background of this whole nefarious business is this. Herodias was the wife of her half-uncle, Herod Philip I; but she left him to marry another half-uncle, his brother Herod Antipas. Herod Antipas was already married to the daughter of Aretas, king of Arabia. Antipas divorced his wife and married Herodias. John the Baptist had condemned this marital musical chairs and had earned the hatred of Herodias who, like Jezebel, was not used to having anyone get in the way of what she wanted. Herodias had forced Antipas to put John in prison, "continually had it in for" John and "kept wanting to kill him" (v. 19). But Herod "kept him safe" in the prison at Machaerus at the southern extremity of his administration just east of the Dead Sea. Herod had a superstitious fear of John, a great respect for his integrity, and even found his conversation uplifting at times ("heard him gladly") when he talked with John at Machaerus. He was also "perplexed" on hearing John because he was torn between John's insistence on right conduct and his devotion to Herodias.

Finally an opportune moment came for Herodias to dispose of John. Herod threw a birthday party for the elite of the governmental, military, and social circles. Herodias' daughter, Salome, danced for the gathering, something that a slave girl rather than a princess normally would do. Herod, apparently heavily plied with wine, was excited by the erotic performance of the girl (about twenty) and made a wild promise to give her whatever she wanted. Salome, not knowing what to ask, left the all-male gathering and went out where her mother and the other women were, to ask advice. Her mother promptly suggested she request the head of John the Baptist. Salome evidently shared her mother's hatred for John and immediately requested the head "on a platter," "at once," lest Herod find a way to weasel out of his promise. Herod was "deeply grieved" but feared to break his oath made before the whole body of dignitaries and acceded to the demand promptly. The way the narrative reads, Salome must have been about as callous as her mother; she calmly made the request and then carried the dish and the head to her mother. John's disciples had access to him in prison (Matt. 11:2ff.) and they were able to get their leader's body and give it a decent burial.

This narrative of John's death records the demise of John, which otherwise would be unknown, accounts for Herod's superstitious ideas about Jesus, reveals the attitude of Herod toward John and Jesus, and introduced here, also dramatically illustrates the cost of discipleship.

Feeding 5,000 (6:30-44). Now Mark picks up the narrative where he left it in verse 13. The "apostles gathered themselves together unto Jesus." The term *apostle* is referred to the Twelve only here in Mark. It is appropriate since the word speaks of one sent on a mission, and they have just returned from theirs. "Gathered themselves together" no doubt means that they came to Jesus two by two until all twelve had collected. There is no hint how long they had been gone, but evidently Jesus had fixed the time and place of return. The apostles gave a complete report of their activities and teaching. Then Jesus, as a wise personnel manager, decided it was time to get away for rest and relaxation and further instruction of His trainees. No doubt the Master Teacher sought to go over numerous experiences with the apostles and show them how they could have been more effective in certain types of circumstances. It was utterly impossible to have an uninterrupted discussion in Capernaum because some were "coming" and others were "going," so there was a constant flow of people and not even "leisure to eat." Therefore He invited them to "come you yourselves in private to an uninhabited place and rest a little" (v. 31). The invitation was only to the Twelve, the place was not desert but simply unpopulated, the duration of the withdrawal was to be brief.

It is clear from Matthew 14:13 that the death of John the Baptist was a tremendously sobering event, calling for reflection on the part of Jesus and His disciples and providing a second reason for a retreat. As a matter of fact, the narrative about John the Baptist hinted that political leaders were becoming increasingly disturbed over the rising popularity of Christ and that a premature crisis was in the offing. Burdick observes that this situation led Jesus to make four withdrawals from Galilee (Mark 6:31-56; 7:24-30; 7:31 - 8:9; 8:10 - 9:50), during which time He concerned Himself with training the Twelve in preparation for His death (p. 1001).

Jesus and the Twelve embarked in "the boat," apparently the same one used in 4:35 and 5:1,21. Periodic reference to "the boat," rather than "a boat," leads to the conclusion that it was one available to the apostolic company virtually on demand and presumably belonged to the partnership of Peter, Andrew, James, and John. According to Luke 9:10, they set sail for the vicinity of Bethsaida, that is Bethsaida Julius, today identified with an unexcavated mound just east of where the Jordan River flows into the Sea of Galilee. The distance was only three to four miles across the top of the Lake of Galilee from Capernaum. Their departure, probably early in the morning, was observed and word quickly spread among the townsfolk. Many "knew" or "understood" what the apostolic company was up to and judged from the direction of the boat about where it would land. So "on foot they ran there together from all the cities." "Ran together" gives the idea that as they ran along others joined the group and swelled its proportions. The reading of the last clause of verse 33 adopted by most translators is "and got there before them." But Lenski observes that there is a variety of textual readings for this clause and argues from John 6:3-5 that Jesus must have arrived first and had at least a brief time with His disciples before the crowd arrived (pp. 261-2).

One should not telescope this account too much. The distance by land was some seven or eight miles. Those who ran were not track stars who had trained for speed or endurance. They would have had to stop periodically for rest and to explain to those in towns along the way what was going on. Moreover, there were all sorts of impediments along the lake shore—boats, nets, houses, fences, marshy land, and the Jordan to ford at the north end of the lake. In addition, Luke 9:11 mentions that Jesus healed many when the crowd did assemble; ill and handicapped could not have moved rapidly. The same would have been true of women and their young children. Perhaps Lenski is right and that the apostolic company had a little time to themselves before the crowd arrived. The King James of verse 34, "when he came out" is closer to the Greek than the versions which talk about disembarking. Possibly Jesus came out of a little declivity or a sheltered spot to view the crowd gathering.

However one interprets all this, the truth is that the crowd did gather and that Jesus was "moved with compassion" as He viewed their obvious needs. Here they were, helpless sheep, with physical and spiritual needs, milling around without satisfactory religious leaders to guide them and to supply those needs. So He began to teach them and to heal many of them (Luke 9:11).

Finally, as the day wore on, the disciples came to Jesus and begged Him to dismiss the crowd so they could go into the villages nearby and purchase food. The time was the first evening according to Matthew 14:15, between 3:00 and 6:00 P.M. Jesus' response was, "You give them to eat." They had no imagination, little memory of divine provision at Cana, and little faith on this occasion. "Shall we go out and buy 200 denarii worth of bread and give it to them?" Probably they didn't have that much (equal to 200 day's pay for a laborer); there would not have been a place to buy it; and they could not have carried it back with them. The situation was impossible.

Then Jesus told them to find out what food was available among the crowd. A lad had five barley loaves and two fish. The loaves were small flat cakes somewhat like pancakes or tortillas; the fish were probably dried or salted. Jesus then commanded that the entire group recline by companies or in groups "on the green grass," indicating it was springtime, near Passover (John 6:4). The crowd obeyed and divided up into "companies" of fifty to 100 each. The word Mark used for companies means *garden beds* and implies that viewed from a distance the whole scene looked like garden beds cut into the grass.

Then speaking a blessing, Jesus broke the cakes and divided the fish and "kept giving" them to the disciples, who then acted as waiters and distributed the food until "all ate" and "were filled." In fact, the disciples collected twelve basketfuls of leftovers, demonstrating the superabundance of the miracle. The baskets were the small wicker variety. The number fed was "5,000 men"; men here is not to be understood as a general word for people but refers to males. Matthew 14:21 indicates there were also women and children. No doubt they were smaller in number and in normal Jewish procedure ate separately.

Walking on the water (6:45-52). The aftermath of this remarkable miracle seems rather strange. Immediately Jesus compelled His disciples to get into the boat and go on ahead to the other side. Meanwhile, He dismissed the crowd and went off into a mountain to pray. It looked as if things were building up to a climax of some sort, but instead there is an anticlimax. John 6:15 provides the explanation. A climax was indeed building. The crowd was so impressed that they wanted to proclaim Him king. The whole divine timetable and plan might have been wrecked. It was a year too early for the triumphal entry. And this was Galilee, not Judea. Jesus had to prevent the action of the crowds, hence His precipitous action.

The feeding of the 5,000 is the only one of the thirty-five miracles of Jesus detailed in the Gospels to be recorded by all four Gospel writers. Perhaps the reason is that it came at the height of His popularity and in connection with the effort to make Him king. Afterward Jesus went off to pray. It was a crucial time in His life when Satan again sought to get Him to bypass the cross, as he had at the temptation when he urged Jesus to fall down and worship him and so receive the kingdoms of this world (Matt. 4:9).

The disciples were ordered to go "to the other side toward Bethsaida" (Mark 6:45), but John 6:17 says toward "Capernaum." Possibly they were slightly east of Bethsaida and were to point the boat in a westerly direction toward Bethsaida as they went to the other side. Or possibly there was another Bethsaida on the western shore of the sea near Capernaum. Clearly they were to head back toward Capernaum.

The time was the second evening (Matt. 14:23), about sunset, as the disciples embarked. Another of those unexpected storms blew up on the Sea of Galilee and the waves began to lash the boat (Matt. 14:24). The disciples took to the oars to stabilize the boat and to try to bring it to shore. But "the wind was contrary to them" and they made almost no progress. Then about the fourth watch of the night, around three in the morning, Jesus came to them, walking on the water. By that time they had covered some three and one-half miles (John 6:19) and must have been nearly exhausted from their efforts. "He meant to go by them." "He wanted the disciples to invite him into the boat. He brought the help so near to them, as it were, offered it to them, but they would receive it only if they desired it and asked for it" (Lenski, p. 274). They thought He was a ghost and shrieked, but He identified Himself: "Cheer up! It is I! Be not afraid!" (At this point occurs the incident of Peter's walking on the water, Matt. 14:28-32.) As soon as Jesus climbed up into the boat the wind stopped, evidently a miraculous event though it is not described as such. Immediately the boat was at its destination (John 6:21). They were only a half mile or so from shore when Jesus came to them. Now the storm was over and they easily came into the dock at Capernaum. "They continued greatly astounded for they did not understand about the loaves"—did not understand that His omnipotence was equally reflected in multiplying the loaves and stilling the sea. "Their hearts were hardened," they were in a state of being spiritually imperceptive.

For the contemporary Christian this incident has a special message. These disciples were in the center of God's will; He had specifically told them to get in the boat and go in the direction they were going. While they were in the center of His will they found themselves in violent distress, and He allowed them to struggle against the storm until they had virtually come to the end of themselves. Then He stepped in and revealed Himself in a new way. This demonstrates the fact that being in God's will does not make one immune to difficulty. In fact, it may lead to extensive testing to perfect one's faith and the appreciation of the power of God.

Gennesaret healing (6:53-56). It seems clear from John 6:22ff. that when Jesus and His disciples completed the journey across the sea they landed at Capernaum, where the Master delivered the discourse on the bread of life. In His audience were some He had fed the day before near Bethsaida. A little later He sailed slightly south of Capernaum along the shore of the plain of Gennesaret (about three miles long and a mile or two wide) and anchored there. If He sought a remote place away from the throngs, He was to be disappointed. As soon as He came out of the boat some "recognized him" and "ran round about the whole region" circulating news of His arrival.

"Began to carry around on their pallets those that were sick where they were hearing that he was." The picture here is of frenzied activity. The people began to carry their sick around on pallets (a bedroll or pad or quilt which four might grasp at the corners, cf. Mark 2); since He moved about, the people had to carry the sick to where He was. If they did not find Jesus in one place, they kept transporting the sick to where they thought they could find Him. Whatever town or village He entered, Jesus always found a crowd and they would place their sick in the market places where He might pass and where they might even touch the border or hem of His robe. "As many as touched him were being made whole." The imperfect tense indicates a rapid succession of cases healed. As with the woman with the issue of blood, so here, healing power flowed from His person in response to faith; there was nothing magical in His clothing.

For Further Study

1. Study the Twelve in chapter 6; their training, experiences, task, development. Do you note any progression or forward step on their part?

2. Study Jesus in this chapter. What do you learn about Him?

3. Compare the two feasts in chapter 6 under such headings as place, guests, master of ceremonies, type of entertainment, etc.

4. Trace on a map the movements made by Jesus and His disciples in Mark 4, 5, and 6.

Chapter 9

Tradition Challenged
(Mark 7:1 – 8:10)

At least three interrelated themes assume increasing prominence as the narrative of Mark continues to unfold: Jesus' rising popularity with the masses leading to the climax at the triumphal entry into Jerusalem; intensifying opposition to Jesus on the part of the religious establishment culminating in the crucifixion; and Jesus' increasing attention to and involvement of the disciples in His ministry until they were completely on their own after the Ascension. In this section, after a magnificent outpouring of popular enthusiasm (6:53-56), the religious leaders launch another of their well-planned attacks on Him, to which Jesus responds with a devastating counterattack on tradition. This is followed by withdrawals to Tyre and Sidon and Decapolis, which include further involvement of the disciples and additional popular interest in His ministry.

Defiled hands (7:1-8). At an indefinite time, possibly weeks after the feeding of the 5,000, a group of Jewish leaders came up from Jerusalem to confront Jesus somewhere in Galilee; perhaps the location was Capernaum. Matthew 15:1 makes it clear that the entire delegation was from Jerusalem and helps in the understanding of Mark 7:1. The scribes were interpreters of the law or specialists in the law or guardians of the law that belonged to the sect of the Pharisees. The Pharisees put great stress on the observance of the law and on rabbinical traditions designed to protect it. In their zeal to protect the law they were constantly expanding or amplifying details of observance. Much of their practice descended into a hollow formalism. They dominated the synagogues of Palestine and had influence among the people far beyond their numbers.

These spies from Jerusalem had seen with their own eyes a violation of the tradition of the elders: some of Jesus' disciples (not all of them nor Jesus Himself) ate with defiled or unwashed hands. This was not a charge that they were guilty of unhygienic personal habits but rather that they did not go through an act of ceremonial cleansing before eating. "They found fault" (KJV) is not in the best manuscripts and should be omitted. In verses 3-4 Mark provides further explanation of pharisaical practices for Roman readers. "Traditions of the elders" consisted of teachings of great rabbis of the past considered binding in common practice. When they came from the marketplace, Pharisees and Jews generally (whom the Pharisees had influenced) ceremonially purified themselves to wash away all defilement. Likewise they ceremonially purified all sorts of other things, including various kinds of utensils. Now the scribes put the question bluntly: "Why do your disciples not walk according to the traditions of the elders?" They held Jesus responsible for the conduct of His disciples and concluded that this one act of the disciples set aside all the traditions of the elders. If one rule was not binding, the rest were not binding, or at least were threatened.

As Jesus responds, He does not defend the disciples but mounts an attack on the Pharisees. First He denounces them on the basis of Scripture. (vv. 6-8). "Well did Isaiah prophecy concerning you." The passage comes from Isaiah 29:13 and is a quotation from the Septuagint version. This translation was a rendition of the Old Testament into Greek in Alexandria about 250-150 B.C. Jesus does not mean to say that Isaiah had the Pharisees primarily in mind when he wrote these words. Rather, their conduct was a fulfillment of the statement Isaiah had uttered concerning his contemporaries, or their actions were a perfect illustration of what Isaiah was talking about. "Hypocrite," a term used only in the Gospels, introduces the idea of an actor under a mask. Originally the word applied to a Greek actor on the stage, one who wore a mask and pretended to be what he was not. "They professed to be followers of God but were in reality followers of men" (Hiebert, p. 175). Their hypocrisy was twofold: their worship and their teachings were empty pretense. His condemnation in the latter case was particularly severe: "teaching as doctrines the precepts of men" (RSV). They were setting forth traditions of the rabbis as if they were the word of God. It should be added that this is a danger in all Christian groups, whether the great confessional churches with their creeds or the less formal churches who require adherence to the views of the bishops of fundamentalism.

Corban (7:9-13). Now Jesus proceeds to denounce the Pharisees by giving an illustration of the results of their position. "You have a beautiful way of nullifying the commandment of God in order that you may keep your tradition!" "Nullify" is in the present tense and is a continuing act; "keep" is in the aorist tense in the Greek, "setting it forth as their deliberate intention to adhere effectively to their tradition" (Hiebert, p. 176). Verse 10a is a statement of the fifth commandment, from Exodus 20:12, while the second half of the verse quotes from Exodus 21:17. Mosaic authorship of these quotations is fully recognized. Although the Mosaic requirement of honoring and supporting one's parents was of divine origin, the Pharisees had a way around the obligation. If one's parents had a need or made a request for something, all he had to do was declare it was corban, that is a gift, or dedicated to God (the temple, etc.), and he no longer had any obligation to father and mother. In this way one could make "null and void the word of God." "And you repeatedly do many things like that," Jesus charged.

Defiled hearts (7:14-23). The Pharisees had charged Jesus' disciples with ceremonial defilement. He had counterattacked by charging them with hypocrisy and with actual nullification of the clear teachings of the Word of God. Now he returns to the subject of defilement and indicates the true source of defilement. But the audience is different. Jesus calls the multitude to Himself again and says, "Pay attention to me, all of you, and understand." "There is nothing outside the man which going into him can defile the man" (v. 15, NASB). Nothing which goes into a person's mouth (food) defiles, but what comes out of one's heart (inner evil nature) does. The Pharisees were still around on the edge of the crowd and heard this saying. They understood the implications and were deeply offended by it (Matt. 15:12), for their view was that food touched by ceremonially unclean hands became unclean and defiled a person eating it.

Without any explanation of the parable, Jesus left the crowd and went into the house, perhaps Peter's in Capernaum, with His disciples. They request further explanation. After expressing surprise at their lack of understanding, Jesus proceeds to give a clear explanation. Food coming from without into an individual does not defile him because it does not enter the heart but goes into the stomach and intestines and the waste passes into the toilet. Thus all foods are clean; none defile morally.

Lenski argues against the translation of the final clause of verse 19 as it appears in several versions—to the effect that Jesus declared all foods clean. Rather, he points out that the verb is in the neuter and that it is the toilet that proves foods clean. He observes, "By being received there the privy shows and proves that the foods never touched the heart at all, never had anything to do with moral defilement, and are thus pronounced clean" (p. 298). Lest it be thought that Jesus had now declared Levitical laws null and void, Lenski observes, ". . . he in no way abrogated the Levitical laws concerning foods. For these laws involved the heart, to transgress them meant to disobey God. . . . All could be eaten as being clean morally as long as the heart was not involved; but the moment the heart disobeyed God in the matter of food the gravest defilement ensued. All Pharisaic regulations had no divine sanction and thus could not involve the heart" (p. 298).

After an implied pause, Jesus turns to what does defile—that which comes out of a person. Out of the heart, i.e., the inner moral nature, proceeds a long list of evil things: evil thoughts (deliberations that stir to action), fornication (unlawful sexual relations), thefts, murders, adultery, covetousness, wickedness (active wickedness), deceit, licentiousness (lascivious-carousing with all lack of restraint), envy (malicious, injurious activity), slander (evil-speaking in general against God and man), pride (against God and man), foolishness (moral senselessness). See the works of the flesh in Galatians 5:19-21.

The Syrophoenician woman (7:24-30). The tide of opposition to Jesus was rising. As noted in the last chapter, Herod Antipas was concerned about Him and wanted to see Him (cf. Luke 9:9). The scribes and Pharisees of Jerusalem and certainly of eastern Galilee were stalking Him and looking for ways to trap Him; He had deeply offended them when He had lectured them about the traditions of the elders (Matt. 15:12). Jesus was not afraid but His work was not yet done, His disciples were not yet trained and He needed rest; so He made another withdrawal during which He could devote Himself more fully to the Twelve. This time He went northwest through the hills of upper Galilee into the borderland of Phoenicia. It does not seem necessary to conclude that he actually ranged through Phoenicia, though He may have crossed the border into it. Although He sought privacy, He could not be hid (v. 24). The reason is at least twofold: in any rural community, information about house guests would spread quickly; and many from the region of Tyre and Sidon had already benefited from His ministry (Mark 3:8).

A certain Gentile (Greek) woman, a Syrophoenician by birth, came to Him as soon as she learned of His whereabouts. Her problem was that her daughter (young but perhaps old enough to be married) was possessed by an unclean spirit and she begged Jesus to cast the demon out of her daughter. He decided to test her faith. First, He did not even answer her (Matt. 15:23). Then He refused her, claiming He was ministering only to Jews. Then He treated her with reproach: "It is not right to take the children's bread and throw it to the dogs" (a term frequently applied to Gentiles). He softened that statement, however; the term He used was not the one for wild dogs of the street but for house pets, "puppies." She accepted that classification and her persistence and faith brought restoration. This is an instance not only of a miracle performed on a Gentile but healing by remote control. Other cases of healing at a distance are the nobleman's son at Capernaum (John 4:46) and the centurion's servant (Luke 7:6). The woman had absolute faith in Jesus' pronouncement of healing and went home to find that it was so.

Healing in Decapolis (7:31-37). "And he went out of the vicinity of Tyre," presumably because the miracle performed there made further privacy impossible. "And he went through Sidon" (preferred reading), definitely spending time in Gentile territory where He would have been unknown. Then the apostolic company made a circuitous route across southern Lebanon around the base of Mount Hermon into Decapolis and eventually to the Sea of Galilee on the east side of the Jordan. Exactly what route they took and how long they spent in transit cannot be guessed. The distance is not great but the terrain is difficult and they were not in a hurry. This was Jesus' peripatetic school. Some believe the tour took several weeks. If so, the question must be raised as to how they supported themselves. They were not known in the area and a hospitable soul would have had to find thirteen beds and to have fed as many hungry mouths. Perhaps the answer is that they paid their own way. It will be remembered that Judas was the treasurer for the group and carried the money box (John 12:6). Numerous women of means, many of whom Jesus had healed, periodically made contributions to His work (Luke 8:2-3).

Somewhere along the way, presumably in Decapolis, a group of friends brought to Jesus for healing a man who was deaf and had a speech impediment (apparently not completely mute, as is often stated). In response, Jesus took the man aside out of public view to avoid publicity and then proceeded to heal him. As is commonly the case, Mark provides graphic details of the scene. Jesus suited symbolic acts to the needs of the unfortunate man. He "shoved" His fingers into his ears to indicate something was to be done about his hearing and then "spat and touched his tongue" to symbolize that his speech was to be restored. The record says only that He spat; it does not say He spat on His finger and then touched it to the man's tongue. If we had fuller records, we might learn that Jesus frequently engaged in symbolic acts when healing individuals. Then He "sighed" or possibly groaned, perhaps as an expression of sympathy, and commanded the organs, "Be opened." Immediately the man's hearing was restored and he "spoke correctly." Not wishing to launch a new healing ministry at this time, Jesus "kept commanding them," the friends, to tell no one. But they paid no attention. The more He told them to be quiet, the more they "heralded" the miracle. The astonishment, apparently of the friends, "exceeded all bounds."

It is of interest to note that following His challenging of the traditions of the Pharisees Jesus has in this chapter healed a Gentile woman's daughter, traveled through Gentile territory, and healed a man in Decapolis, which was also predominately Gentile. Perhaps Mark has grouped these events together to underscore Jesus' contest with the Pharisees and His willingness to do things that overly legalistic Pharisees would not do.

Feeding 4,000 (8:1-10). "In those days," presumably refers to the same general time indicated in the last chapter. Evidently Jesus was on His way to the Sea of Galilee when the crowd formed that He fed on this occasion, because after the miracle was performed Jesus and His disciples got into a boat to cross the Sea of Galilee. The publicity given the healing of the deaf man with the speech impediment easily could have caused the crowd to gather.

Liberals commonly assume that the feeding of the 4,000 is merely a variant of the earlier feeding of the 5,000. Since only Matthew and Mark mention the miracle, while all four Gospels report the feeding of the 5,000, only two writers then would be guilty of the mistake. A reverent view of Scripture cannot permit acceptance of such a conclusion. And a careful study of the two miracles shows that although there are some similarities, the differences require accepting these as two separate events. By means of a simple chart the differences become evident and the salient details of the present narrative become clear.

Feeding 5,000	*Feeding 4,000*
Crowd from west and north shore of Sea of Galilee	Crowd from northeast of Sea of Galilee
Crowd with Jesus one day	Crowd with Him three days
Compassion of Jesus primarily for spiritual reasons	Compassion primarily because of physical need
Event is somewhere on east or northeast shore of Sea in an uninhabited place	Event is on east or northeast of Sea in an uninhabited place
Food available: five loaves and two fish, belonging to a boy in crowd	Food available: seven loaves and a few fish, presumably belonging to disciples
Crowd is seated	Crowd is seated
Jesus blesses food and multiplies it	Jesus blesses food and multiplies it
Disciples distribute food	Disciples distribute food
Crowd is satisfied—filled with food	Crowd is filled
Leftovers: twelve small wicker baskets full	Leftovers: seven hamper-size baskets full
5,000 men, plus women and children eat	4,000 men, besides women and children eat (cf. Matt. 15:38)
Crowd responded by wanting to make Jesus king	No response known. If Gentiles, they would have had no messianic vision
Jesus sent the crowd away	Jesus sent the crowd away
Jesus sent the disciples away in a boat and He went off to pray	Jesus and the disciples sailed in a boat together
Destination of disciples: Capernaum	Destination: Dalmanutha, location uncertain but was on western side of Sea of Galilee

One additional comment is necessary. Some commentators feel that if this were a second miracle of feeding, the disciples should have picked up a cue from the previous miracle and suggested another miracle. Such commentators are very critical of the Twelve. But Plummer does not interpret this response as a complete lack of faith and says, ". . . they confess their own powerlessness and leave the solution to Him . . . Moreover, Christ does not rebuke them" (p. 195), which is what we would expect if they were too spiritually dull.

For Further Study

1. What might the disciples have learned in Mark 7:1 - 8:10?

2. Study the three miracles introduced in this section, noting Jesus' method; responses to them by the subjects, observers, or disciples; that over which Jesus had power in performing each.

3. Show how Jesus used Scripture, illustration, and logic in answering the Pharisees.

4. What do you learn about Jesus' outlook and attitudes from His conduct and conversation in this section?

Chapter 10

Sight and Insight
(Mark 8:11-30)

In this passage first the Pharisees and then the disciples demonstrate lack of insight. Subsequently a man of Bethsaida receives his sight and Peter evidences true insight as he utters the great confession.

Pharisees seek sign (8:11-13). "And the Pharisees came out and began to dispute with him." Opposition to Jesus continues to move toward a climax as now the Pharisees team up with their enemies the Sadducees (Matt. 16:1) to accost Jesus. Opposites of the Pharisees in almost every way, the Sadducees were of the priestly party and represented the aristocracy. They all "came out," apparently from wherever they were in Capernaum when Jesus returned to that town. They requested a "sign from heaven," some sort of miracle that would demonstrate beyond a shadow of a doubt that He was the Messiah (probably something at least as great as Elijah's causing fire to fall from heaven). Of course this demand rejected the adequacy of miracles already performed and called for a great show of power they did not think He could produce. And they could always reject any new miracle as insufficient to prove His messiahship.

What they were "tempting him" to do was to "make himself a messiah after the fashion of men so as to gain their favor and support by self-chosen means" (Lenski, p. 321) and thus were suggesting something of the same sort that Satan tempted Him to do during the temptation in the wilderness. He "sighed deeply," perhaps at the hardness of their hearts and the realization that the opposition was reaching crisis proportions and the time when He would bear the sin of mankind on the crass was inching nearer. "Why does this generation seek a sign?" Certainly not so they may believe, but only to discredit. He refused their request, but Matthew (16:4) adds that they would have the sign of the prophet Jonah—the sign of His resurrection. Then He left the Pharisees and Sadducees and sailed with His disciples to the other side of the Sea of Galilee. They probably sailed from Capernaum and evidently headed for Bethsaida (v. 22).

Lesson concerning leaven (8:14-21). As they disembarked they discovered they had forgotten to take along any food and had only one bread-cake in the boat (Matt. 16:5). As they commented on the problem, Jesus used the occasion to issue a warning against the leaven of the Pharisees and Herod (the whole religious aristocracy of Herodians and Sadducees). This He meant to apply to the corrupting power of the teaching of the Pharisees and Herod. The disciples did not get the point at all but thought He was in some way referring to their failure to bring along something to eat. Then He proceeded to raise questions concerning the feeding of the 5,000 and the 4,000, evidently to show them that He could not be talking about the problem of their lack of food. After all, He had fed the multitudes *and them* and He could do so again. Matthew 16:12 shows that under Jesus' teaching the disciples finally came to understand what He was talking about, so the answer to the question of verse 21, "Do you now understand?" is, Yes.

Before leaving this scene it is important to note that leaven is yeast, which has the function of breaking down cells in the bread, of permeating the entire substance and changing its essential character. The corrupting influence of the Pharisees was their false holiness and of the Sadducees (Herodians) their denial of the supernatural and their humanistic view of religion.

Men as trees (8:22-26). The crossing of the Lake of Galilee evidently began another of Jesus' withdrawals with His disciples. Though they had started out for an uninhabited place, their failure to take along food necessitated a trip into town—Bethsaida. This Bethsaida Julias, built up by Herod Philip in honor of Julia, the daughter of Augustus Caesar, now became the scene of another miracle. After the feeding of the 5,000 nearby, Jesus was known here and some people brought a blind man to Him for healing. Jesus took the man by the hand and led him out of town and then proceeded to use symbolic acts in the process of healing as He had with the man who was deaf and had a speech impediment. He spit on the man's eyes and put his fingers on them, indicating that something was happening. Then He asked the man if he saw anything, a question that would require him to open his eyes and observe that something was happening to him. The fact that the man could compare people to trees walking around (knowing what both looked like) and the fact that his sight was "restored" (v. 25) indicates he had not been blind from birth but had lost his eyesight some years later. Why Jesus chose to accomplish this healing in stages we do not know; perhaps the process provided a thrilling experience for the patient. At any rate, the man "saw everything clearly" and was fully restored. Then Jesus sent him away to his home, commanding him not even to enter Bethsaida. Evidently he lived outside of the town and probably the full significance of what happened to him would best be appreciated in the quiet of his home rather than in the din of the mob.

Who am I? (8:27-30). "And Jesus went out and his disciples into the villages of Caesarea Philippi." Jesus and the Twelve went north from Bethsaida some twenty-five miles to the vicinity of Caesarea Philippi. Herod Philip built this city at the site of Paneas and named it for Tiberius Caesar. Then to distinguish it from Caesarea on the seacoast, he attached his own name to it. The place was a Gentile center but the villages around it were not as largely so. Jesus apparently stayed in the villages. At the foot of Mount Hermon, the region was beautiful and rustic; one of the sources of the Jordan flowed nearby.

On the road north Jesus elicited from the disciples a response to the question of how people were identifying Him. He did this not to obtain information but to lead them to express the Great Confession. They reported the same ideas that Herod Antipas and others were expressing according to Mark 6:14-15: John the Baptist, Elijah, and one of the prophets. All of these views were good, but they failed to include the concept of messiahship. As over against these views of the masses Jesus said, "But you, whom do you say that I am?" placing them in a separate category. Apparently rather promptly Peter said, "You are the Christ" or the anointed one or the Messiah. Matthew (16:16) adds, "the Son of the living God," which indicates he also accepted the full deity of Christ. And Jesus responded then with the reward for his faith in Matthew 16:17-19. Mark's abbreviated statement probably reflects Peter's humility; he would let others cast him in a more significant role. Evidently the rest of the Twelve assented to Peter's declaration.

This was not a new thought to the disciples. After all, John the Baptist had presented Him as such to at least Peter and Andrew at the beginning of their discipleship and all of them probably had accepted the idea long before. But it was essential that they make an oral affirmation as opposition mounted and He prepared to enter the Passion period of His life.

We cannot be fully sure what the Twelve meant by a declaration of messiahship. In the century or two before the birth of Christ Jews had come to attach political aspirations to the messianic concept and Old Testament references to a suffering servant (e.g., Isa. 53) were largely ignored. Probably the disciples also were expecting Him to set up a political kingdom. This must have been the hope of Judas; James and John wanted to sit on His right and His left in the kingdom; Peter was unprepared for the passion announcement (v. 32) and opposed the thought of His death. After Peter's (the disciples') confession, Jesus "gave them strict orders" to tell no one about His true identity. Not only would this inflame the general populace who had purely nationalistic hopes, but the disciples themselves were not yet ready to proclaim the true nature of His messiahship, for they did not understand the significance of the cross.

For Further Study

1. In Matthew's account of Jesus' response to Peter's confession, the Master uttered an elevated prophecy or reward. How would you interpret Matthew 16:17-19?

2. With the help of an unabridged concordance and a Bible dictionary or encyclopedia, make a study of leaven in Scripture.

3. What was there in Jesus' teaching and conduct that would have led people to conclude that He was John the Baptist? Elijah? a prophet?

Chapter 11

Preview of Passion and Glory
(Mark 8:31 – 9:29)

First passion announcement (8:31 - 9:1). The first passion announcement appears in Mark 8:31, and from this point onward the cross will be increasingly on the mind of Christ and increasingly in the spotlight in Mark's narrative. The last major part of the book may be said to begin here. "And he began to teach them that it was necessary that the Son of man suffer." Other announcements of the passion would follow. "That it was necessary" reveals that it was part of the divine plan for His life— part of God's plan for mankind's redemption. "Many things" is left general for the moment. His rejection would come at the hands of the "elders" (lay leaders), "chief priests" (Sadducees), and "scribes" (Pharisees)—the three groups in the Sanhedrin, the chief council of the Jews. Furthermore, He would "be killed" and "after three days rise again." This latter thought was incomprehensible to the Twelve. So there would be no mistake or lack of clarity in their minds, He "kept saying this statement [repeatedly] openly and without disguise."

Only hints of His death had come several times earlier: (1) John the Baptist had pointed to Him as the Lamb of God who would take away the sin of the world (John 1:29); (2) in Jerusalem He had spoken of a temple to be destroyed and rebuilt in three days (John 2:19); (3) to Nicodemus He had said the Son of man would be lifted up as the serpent in the wilderness (John 3:12-16); (4) to His disciples He had said the bridegroom would be taken away (Matt. 9:15); (5) in the Capernaum synagogue He had declared He was about to give His flesh for the life of the world (John 6:47-51).

"But Peter," who had just made such a noble confession, took Him by the hand or perhaps put his hand on the Master's shoulder, drew Him aside a little, and began to remonstrate with Him. He found the idea of a suffering Messiah abhorrent. Presumably Peter was standing at Jesus' side speaking in His ear. When Jesus turned around to face Peter, He saw the rest of the disciples standing there, perhaps approving Peter's sentiments. In full view of them all He rebuked Peter: "Get behind me, Satan," get out of My way, you are an instrument of Satan, trying to dissuade Me from becoming the Redeemer. Satan also had wanted Him to accept the kingdom without the cross (Matt. 4:8-10). "You do not have in mind the things of God, but the things of men" (NIV). You do not understand God's plan for dealing with the sin problem of the world through the death of Christ, but as men do, you view Christ as a person of great power who could set up His rule among men without suffering.

Jesus had just said something about bearing His own cross. Now He proceeded to declare that there is a cross for His disciples to bear also. At this juncture Jesus called to Himself a crowd that evidently had been gathering, probably Jews of the area, and addressed them along with the Twelve. The subject is not salvation but discipleship. "If anyone wills to come after me, he must deny himself and take up his cross and keep on following me." "Deny" and "take up" are both aorist imperatives in the Greek and are commands to perform a single definite crisis act; a comparable concept is "present" in Romans 12:1.

To deny self is to take self off the throne, to turn away from self-centeredness and to become Christ-centered instead. It does not mean that one deliberately browbeats self, puts on some false act of humility, becomes careless about his person, or denies a God-given personality. A truly Christ-centered person may work hard on personal appearance so as to be winsome for the sake of Christ or may work hard on enunciation, word usage, and the like in order to be more effective in the ministry. There is nothing wrong with giving careful attention to self, provided that the reason for doing so is the glory of God. Crossbearing is not enduring some illness or other such burden in life, but applies to the trials which come to the believer because of his Christian profession and which can be escaped by denying the obligation of discipleship. The last verb in the verse is in the present tense and involves continuing action, persevering obedience.

This mention of the cross is revealing indeed and shows what was on Jesus' mind. He had just made a passion announcement but had given no hint of the manner in which He would die or that it would be at anyone's hands but the Jews. Now He talked about a Roman means of execution in describing discipleship; and of course He would be the leader of all who would follow Him. "Whoever wants to save his [physical] life" and ignores the claims of Christ may do so, but he will miss the life that is eternal or miss the fuller life. "Whoever is willing to lose his life," either in the sacrifice of personal ambition or wealth or martyrdom for the sake of Christ or the promulgation of His message (the gospel), will find it, safe and blessed with God.

Verse 36 is susceptible to two interpretations. If one spends all of life only trying to amass a fortune and build a reputation, what good is it? He dies and can no longer enjoy it. Or what is the worth of collecting earthly treasure only if it means forfeiting the higher life or sacrificing eternal life? In either case the negative result is the same. The soul is of incomparable value (v. 37) and is worth all the sacrifice one makes here on earth to save it or nurture it. "Whoever is ashamed of me and my words," whoever refuses to accept the Messiah and His message and the demands of discipleship in this generation of people unfaithful to God will likewise suffer being disowned by the Messiah when He comes back in power.

Jesus had foretold His crucifixion and resurrection, and in the parabolic statement about the bridegroom, His departure from the disciples. Now He introduces the concept of His return—not as a meek and lowly person subjecting Himself to the machinations of His enemies, but as one who shares all the glory of the Father. And this coming will be with dignity and power, as underscored by His entourage of holy angels. The prediction that some present would not die before they saw Him come in His glory is most naturally interpreted to refer to the three members of the inner circle who shortly were to witness the glorified Christ at the Transfiguration, which was a foretaste of the coming of Christ and His kingdom.

The Transfiguration (9:2-8). Six days after the first passion announcement Jesus took Peter, James, and John up into a high mountain to pray (Luke 9:28). Since they were in the vicinity of Caesarea Philippi, in the shadow of Mount Hermon, the most natural conclusion is that they went up on a spur of that mountain. Then "he was transfigured before them." Transfigured is the translation of a word from which we get metamorphosis. Thus He experienced an essential change of form, not merely of appearance, and actually assumed the glorified form He will have at His second coming. Mark makes an effort to describe the scene; he alone uses the term "glistening" to portray the impression made by Jesus' garments. In the classics the word applies to a flashing sword, sunshine on shields, or the blinding whiteness of a flash of lightning. Mark observes that the appearance of His clothes was whiter than it was possible to produce by any process known to man. Elijah and Moses appeared with Jesus. These two may represent the law and the prophets, and both of them left this life under unusual circumstances (God buried Moses secretly and He raptured Elijah). Elijah may have been mentioned first here and may have been chosen as a representative of the prophets because the scribes expected his return as a forerunner of Messiah. "And they were talking with Jesus" about His decease at Jerusalem (Luke 9:31). What a conversation on which to eavesdrop!

The three disciples "became terrified." But as Moses and Elijah were about to leave (Luke 9:33), Peter felt he had to respond to the situation. "It is good for us to be here; let us make three booths"; presumably he wanted to prolong the event, as making a place of repose would be sure to do. What a contrast: indescribable glory sheltered in crude makeshift huts of wattled boughs. It was obvious that Peter, like the others, was so overcome by the situation that "he did not know how to respond" (v. 6). While Peter was still speaking a bright cloud apparently enveloped them all (Matt. 17:5; Luke 9:34). Out of the cloud came the voice of the Father, giving witness to the Son as at the baptism. When the cloud lifted Jesus was alone with the disciples. The question arises, why the transfiguration and why at this point in time? Evidently it was part of the training of the disciples, helping them to understand who Jesus really was and providing a foregleam of glory that would help to tide them over the dark days of crucifixion and the subsequent period of waiting before Pentecost. It was important to Jesus too and provided Him with a taste of the glory that had been His and would again be His. This reminder would buoy Him up also as He endured the indescribable sufferings of the passion (Heb. 12:2 may be relevant here). The event logically occurs here right after the first passion announcement.

Elijah is come (9:9-13). As they came down the mountain the next day (Luke 9:37), Jesus put a seal on their lips, absolutely forbidding them to reveal the wonders they had just seen until after the resurrection of Jesus. Tales of this sort would only inflame the masses into a premature proclamation of the messianic reign. Committed to silence on one point, they had plenty to talk about on another—the meaning of the Resurrection. They believed in the future resurrection of the dead and Jesus had plainly told them of His resurrection in the first passion announcement. But the concept of the Messiah in Judaism in general was of a reigning king, and the Transfiguration had presented Him in His glory. They could not quite fit in the idea of resurrection. Something else they could not figure out concerned Elijah. The scribes had taught on the basis of Malachi 4:5 that Elijah must return before the coming of Messiah. Jesus made it clear (v. 13) that Elijah did indeed come, evidently in the person of John the Baptist. His restoration of all things (v. 12) must have reference to his spiritual preparation for the Messiah. In the midst of His answer to the Twelve, Jesus also called attention to Old Testament prophecies concerning the suffering of the Messiah (e.g., Isa. 53); they were just as real a part of the prophetic teaching concerning Messiah as the fact that Elijah's coming must precede His.

The demonic boy (9:14-29). Jesus and Peter, James, and John now arrived at the place where the other nine were engaged in a dispute with some scribes in the presence of a crowd of people. Apparently the dispute was over why the nine did not have the power to deliver a demon-possessed boy. Jesus immediately asked the scribes why they were arguing with the disciples, and the father of the boy told the reason. A demon had rendered the boy deaf and dumb and periodically it threw him into convulsions resembling epileptic fits or worse. Jesus upbraided the disciples for their lack of faith. Evidently verse 19 was not addressed to the crowd or to the father who came in faith but to the disciples who because of their lack of faith were helpless.

Jesus now commanded that the boy be brought to Him. At once the demon was so troubled that it threw the boy into a fit. At this juncture Jesus engaged the father in conversation, probably for the purpose of demonstrating the hopelessness of the situation. In verse 22 the father indicated a lapse of faith, "if you can do anything." His faith probably had flagged with the setback already experienced. Now Jesus proceeded to strengthen his faith: "all things are possible for him who believes." One must not conclude he can have just anything he wishes by faith. Lenski pointedly observes, "But 'all things' are here concrete: all those things which faith trusts to the power of Jesus who, moreover, always exerts power and ability according to his good and gracious will" (p. 381). With a loud burst of emotion the father yelled out, apparently sobbing violently, "I do believe; help my unbelief."

At this juncture, with the lad lying on the ground in convulsions, Jesus observed that the crowd which apparently had been dispersing started to form again. So He quickly proceeded to the healing. He commanded the spirit to come out and not to return. The unclean spirit then threw the boy into terrible contortions and left. Most of those standing around thought the boy dead but Jesus restored him fully.

Later the disciples inquired about their inability to cast out the demon. Jesus' answer was that "this kind," particularly difficult to expel, could be driven out only through prayer. In various places in the New Testament it is clear that there are classes of demons or differences among them; some are worse than others. Evidently what happened in this case was that when the demon refused to come out the disciples had admitted defeat instead of going to God in believing prayer for the necessary enablement to perform the miracle. They had taken the power of God for granted and had not maintained an open channel to the continued flow of His power.

For Further Study

1. What did the Transfiguration mean to Jesus? to the disciples?

2. How do the incidents in this section relate to each other; why is each included?

3. Is there evidence of change in any of the disciples in this section?

4. Note at least five contrasts in this section.

Chapter 12

Greatness in Humble Service
(Mark 9:30 – 10:52)

The title chosen for this section aptly highlights its contents. On two occasions the Twelve discussed which of them would be greatest in the kingdom (9:33-37; 10:35-45), but Jesus stressed servanthood as the way to greatness (9:35). He talked about rewards for humble service (9:41) and the fact that entrance into the kingdom must come by childlike faith (10:15). The rich and those of high position have nothing special to recommend them to God; in fact, riches are a hindrance to faith. But preeminently, in two passion announcements (9:30-32; 10:32-34), Jesus pointed to His own service in giving His life a ransom for the sins of mankind (10:45).

Second passion announcement (9:30-32) "And they went out from there"; the apostolic group left the vicinity of Caesarea Philippi, probably because the healing of the demonic boy made them too well known and Jesus wanted to be alone with the Twelve. They "kept moving" along through Galilee, evidently bypassing the larger towns because Jesus wanted to travel unnoticed so He could teach the Twelve. The startling truth is that His Galilean ministry was over. He "kept teaching" and "kept saying" to them. He repeatedly taught them the truth of His passion. This announcement differed little from the earlier one (8:31). The only real difference is the prediction that He would "be delivered [possibly a hint of the betrayal] into the hands of men" (possibly an indication that more than Jews were to be involved). But they still did not really understand what He was trying to tell them. Judaism so fully expected a kingly Messiah that they could not comprehend the idea of the Suffering Servant. Moreover, there is a revealing clause in Luke 9:45 to the effect that there was a certain divine blinding that kept them from a full understanding of what He was telling them. As to the reason for that, Hiebert ventures, "In the providence of God, their failure to understand was overruled to spare them the agony of the prospect of the Passion" (p. 226). Afraid to ask for further elucidation, lest they be condemned for their dullness, they remained in their ignorance.

First discussion on greatness (9:33-37). When the group arrived in Capernaum, they remained in seclusion and Jesus continued to teach them, first on the question of true greatness. "The house" was probably the house of Peter. "He kept asking them, 'What were you arguing about on the way?'" He couldn't pry out of them what the topic of their heated debate had been; they were too embarrassed. Well they might have been for in the context of Jesus' effort to impress on them His coming suffering they had been discussing which of them was (were) the greatest among the company. Evidently Jesus' singling out three of them for special attention caused friction that could not be eliminated easily.

Of course they did not have to tell Him what they had been talking about; He knew. As the authoritative rabbi, He sat down and called the disciples for a heart-to-heart talk. To instruct them properly, first He stated a principle: "If anyone wants to be first [in the kingdom], he must choose to be last of all and willing servant of all." He must be characterized by humility and a willingness to serve. Then He proceeded to teach them symbolically. He took a child, perhaps Peter's who was playing around the house, and stood him in the middle of the group with His arms around him. And again He stated a principle: "Whoever receives one of such little children [such a trusting, dependent person] in my name [on the basis of the revelation of Jesus one has received] receives me [an act done to Christ Himself]," and receives not Him alone "but him who commissioned me." This simple act of receiving a little child and ministering to him in the name of Jesus, or by extension, serving a humble disciple of Jesus, involves reception of the Father and elevates us as nothing else can.

Service by an outsider (9:38-41). At this juncture John broke in with a question, undoubtedly prompted by Jesus' teaching that whoever does good deeds in His name pleases Him and the Father. The Twelve had met a man casting out demons in Jesus' name and "tried to hinder him [but were not able to stop him] because he was not following us." Evidently their concern in trying to stop the man was not professional pride but involved the question of whether those outside the company and not under Jesus' tutelage had the right to use His name in exorcism. Jesus said, "Stop hindering him," and observed that it was impossible for anyone actually doing supernatural acts in the name of or on the authority of Jesus to be opposed to Him. He might have repeated part of the teaching given earlier that "Satan cannot cast out Satan." Therefore, "he who is not against us is for us." He who is for Jesus is also for His disciples. Whoever performs acts of kindness for you because you belong to Christ, and for His sake, he will receive a reward for the token of devotion to Him.

Offending members (9:42-50). This last paragraph in the chapter may refer to Jesus' teaching about children or His answer to John. "Whoever shall put a stumbling block [impediment] in the way of one of these little ones who believe in me" may apply to young children or the lowliest believer or immature believers, or any servant of Christ referred to in John's question. It would be better for such a one to have a millstone, a large stone turned by a donkey in grinding grain, hanged about his neck and he be thrown into the sea. He would be better dead than alive and a hindrance to other believers.

Then in verses 43-48 attention turns to the danger of causing one's self to stumble. The meaning of the passage is that anything that ensnares a person and causes him to fall into sin should be cut off. The hand, foot, and eye cannot really cause one to stumble by itself for each is directed by the evil heart to act in sinful ways. So it is necessary to change the heart if one is to be saved. And the three members must be symbolic of things to be cut away. Perhaps, as Hiebert has suggested, the hands stand for things one does, the feet for places one goes, and the eye for stimuli that come from the outside (pp. 232-33). One may have to practice radical surgery in all these areas to prevent being destroyed by the temptations in each area. It is better to go into "the life," eternal life "maimed," with incomplete enjoyment of all one's senses than to go into "Gehenna," destroyed by full enjoyment of them.

Ge-Hinnom, the valley of the Hinnom, south of Jerusalem, was a place of pagan worship under the apostate kings Ahaz and Manasseh. The good king Josiah defiled it and turned it into the city dump (2 Kings 23:10). Worms lived in the garbage and fires frequently were lit to burn the rubbish. Hence it became a picture of the place of the wicked dead, who would suffer from external punishment (fire) and internal torment (worms). Verse 48 teaches that this suffering was to be eternal. Verses 44 and 46 do not appear in the best manuscripts and probably should be omitted. But verse 48 is certainly genuine.

The last two verses are difficult. The last half of verse 49 as it appears in the King James Version apparently is not genuine; so the verse should read, "For everyone will be salted with fire." Commentators present divergent interpretations but there is not room here for all their variations. Probably the reference is to the disciples who would be purified (as salt purifies) by fire (the work of the Holy Spirit and the Word in the life as they burn away the dross). The disciples are warned against becoming unbelieving and worldly again (against becoming "saltless") and are commanded "to have salt in yourselves" (purifying power) and "be at peace with each other" (don't let the ambition for earthly greatness disturb your peaceful relations, see v. 33).

Galilee to Judea (10:1). "Rising up from there," Jesus now makes a clean break with Galilee. The first eleven chapters of Mark focused mainly on Jesus' Galilean ministry; the rest of the book will center on His Judean ministry. Between Mark 9:50 and 10:1 the author omits the events of Luke 9 - 19 and John 7 - 11, many of which are of Jewish interest and not especially germane to Mark's Gentile orientation. "And went through the region of Judea and the other side of the Jordan" is equivalent to saying "through Judea and Perea." It is not clear whether Mark means to say that Jesus went to Judea directly from Galilee and then made a side trip to Perea or whether Judea was the goal and he went through Perea on the way south. In any case, chapter 10 describes a series of events during Jesus' last journey to Jerusalem and the Passion Week. After some months of retirement when Jesus had been especially giving Himself to the training of His disciples, He "again" makes Himself available to the multitudes and "again" teaches them, as He was accustomed to doing. The mention of "crowds" indicates that Jesus was popular in Judea and Perea as in Galilee.

The divorce question (10:2-12). As Jesus was teaching (probably in Perea) some Pharisees stepped forth from the crowd to ask a question about divorce. Clearly their motive was to "test" or trip Him. Perhaps they hoped to get Him to contradict Moses, or embroil Him in controversy between the prevailing rabbinical schools of thought on the subject, or to get Him in trouble with Herod Antipas as had been the case with John the Baptist, or to entangle Him in some inconsistency in His own argument. Apparently their fuller statement of the question appears in Matthew 19:3: "Is it lawful for a man to put away his wife for every cause?" The Jewish background is this. Two rabbinical positions had developed in the interpretation of Deuteronomy 24:1: that of Shammai who said divorce was lawful on grounds of infidelity alone, and that of Hillel who permitted it on the basis of numerous slight provocations.

As He did frequently, Jesus responded to His interrogators with a question of His own, "What did Moses command you?" In His reply Jesus demonstrated His orthodoxy in appealing to Moses and at the same time reminded the Pharisees of their ultimate basis of authority. The Pharisees responded, "Moses permitted a man to write a certificate of divorce and send her away" (NIV). Of course Moses did not command divorce; but if there was to be a divorce, there had to be an official writ of divorce. Thus relationships would be publicly recognized and regularized and the evil of temporary purely personal liaisons eliminated. Jesus then explained that Moses wrote this command in their law because of their moral perversity.

Then He proceeded to go back of the Mosaic law to a higher law in the divine order of creation. God did not originally intend that the marriage relations should be broken at all, but sin had entered human history and had made havoc of the relationship; hence Moses had made a concession to evil. Certainly Moses was not altering God's original intention of the permanency of the marriage tie. God Himself made a male and female, complementary to each other, and brought them together. "For this reason a man shall leave behind [abandon] his father and mother and be glued to his wife, and the two shall be one flesh." Marriage involves three facets: cutting off parental ties, commitment to a life partner, and a sexual relationship that binds the two permanently in one. If any one of these elements is lacking a marriage is in trouble. Especially is the first point to be underscored. Many marriages founder because parents are too involved in the day to day decision-making process of a young couple.

If the man and woman are "no longer two but one flesh," then the Pharisees were wrong in thinking the two were so loosely joined that the husband could easily send his wife away. "What God has joined together, man must not separate." The union was divine; it was the aim of creation. Divorce is purely human. After a pronouncement like this the Pharisees were thoroughly silenced. They made no further recorded comments. Evidently Jesus' fuller teaching on the subject did permit divorce on grounds of adultery (see Matt. 19:3-9). Infidelity did in fact destroy the unity and a writ of divorce merely attested the dissolution of the union.

Apparently Jesus went on to make the further point of Mark 10:10-12 in the presence of the Pharisees (Matt. 19:9), but the disciples asked Him "again" later on "in the house." Jesus now envisioned the fact that divorced persons will remarry; as a matter of fact, they were commonly getting divorced so they could remarry. To such He observed that men who remarry commit adultery against their former mates. Divorced women likewise are regarded as adulterous if they remarry. "If she divorces her husband." A Jewish woman could not divorce her husband, though she could persuade her husband to divorce her. Evidently verse 12 anticipates a time when the gospel would reach out to the Gentile world (where either partner could initiate a divorce) and is especially included here for Roman readers. So if persons are divorced they are not to remarry. There is not room here to discuss the whole question of divorce and remarriage.[1] Perhaps a thought that Jesus Himself introduced at the end of the parallel passage in Matthew 19:11 opens up the question somewhat: "All men cannot receive this saying." It is worth asking whether this verse may permit some courses of action "because of the hardness of men's hearts."

Blessing the children (10:13-16). Though Jesus is now available to the crowds once more, evidently He is still very much concerned with training the Twelve. He spoke to them privately on the divorce question and now He has specific things to say about their attitude toward the children. Evidently Jesus is still in the house while this event takes place. As parents "kept bringing" little children, the disciples stood outside and "kept rebuking" them and tried to turn them away. There is no need to view the disciples as gruff, ungracious men. Perhaps they already saw the tenstion evident in Jesus' demeanor as He approached Calvary. Perhaps they wanted to spare the Master this added burden and intrusion on His privacy. Perhaps they wanted more of His time for instruction. If most of the "young children" were babes in arms, it may be easier to understand the disciples' frustration. Should He not be spending His time with older persons who had greater understanding and greater need? It is impossible to determine from the Greek, however, that all or most of the children were merely babes. When Jesus saw the hindering efforts of the disciples, He was indignant and

---

[1] A brief discussion of the subject may be found in Charles C. Ryrie, *You Mean the Bible Teaches That*, Chicago: Moody Press, 1974. See also John Murray, *Divorce*, Philadelphia: Orthodox Presbyterian Church, 1953.

immediately gave the order to "stop hindering them."

And then He gave the spiritual significance or symbolism of the moment: "for the kingdom of God belongs to such as these" (NASB) and "Whoever does not receive the kingdom of God as a little child shall not enter into it." "Such as these" does not mean that all children can count on belonging to the kingdom of God, but certain childlike qualities must characterize the true children of the kingdom. Barclay itemizes these as humility, tendency to obedience, trust (acceptance of authority and confidence), and a short memory when it comes to bearing grudges (pp. 250-51). In spite of all the pressures upon Him, Jesus took up the children in His arms and "kept on fervently blessing them." There was nothing perfunctory in this ministry of the Savior. He must have been a kindly person, with a gracious smile and an ability to laugh with those who were having fun. And the true greatness of the Master is seen once more in His humble service as He blessed the "least of these."

Quest for eternal life (10:17-22). The characteristic of Mark as a Gospel of action is certainly evident in this account of a rich man. Just as Jesus was in the act of taking the road to the next town, a man came running to Him in eagerness to learn His secret of eternal life and knelt to Him in profound respect. From Matthew we learn that he was young (19:20,22) and from Luke that he was a ruler (18:18)—of what is not clear. Commonly it is assumed that he was a ruler of a synagogue, but if so he should have been older. In any case, he was a man of wealth and position and uprightness of character.

The question he asks is in marked contrast to the point that Jesus had just been making in the house: receiving the kingdom of God as a little child. His question is, "What must I *do* to get eternal life?" He does not ask *how*, as if he were in any doubt as to the method, but "*what* must I *do*" to make up whatever is lacking in human performance. He does sense that something is lacking, even though he has been careful to keep the law, or he would never have come in the first place. Lenski observes: "His conception of Jesus is thus much like that of the modernists: Jesus is a man who has discovered the good thing and by it found eternal life. His essential Sonship as also his atonement are brushed aside. The only question is: 'Lord, how didst thou do it? Tell us that we may do likewise'" (p. 430).

"Why do you call me good?" Jesus answered. "No one is good—except God alone" (v. 19). Commentators often conclude that Jesus was indicating His own deity here. If the young man called Him "good" and only God is good, then did the young man accept the idea that Jesus was God? Such commentators may be right, but the emphasis in this verse seems rather to be on the fact that only God is good, human beings are not. The way to God is not to discover from another human being his secret of how to live a good life in order to *earn* God's favor, but rather to come in faith to God, who alone can bestow eternal life. Then Jesus sought to deal with the rich young ruler on the basis on which he had come—law works. He reminded him of the obligation of the law and noted the last half of the ten commandments, which deal with human relationships.

The ruler responded, "all these I have watched from my youth on." Ever since age twelve, when according to Jewish practice he had assumed the yoke of the commandments, he had been scrupulous to observe the letter of the law and to keep it inviolate. He felt he was blameless in this regard. But he knew something was still missing, for according to Matthew 19:20 he asked, "What lack I yet?"

Jesus looked at him with that penetrating look that perhaps Peter (who influenced Mark in his writing) knew best (Luke 22:61). Then He "began to love him"—to show toward him an unselfish desire to help the man in his deplorable condition. "In one thing you lag behind" evidently refers to a failure to put God first in his life and/or to exercise a true and saving faith in Christ. In other words, while he may have been blameless in regard to the second part of the Ten Commandments, he was not in regard to the first part. The man's earthly possessions had usurped the place of God in his heart. That is why the test "go, sell, give" is administered in this case.

This form of sacrifice is not demanded of all, but the right attitude toward possessions is. As Cole aptly observes, "Christ demands of us an initial renunciation of all, when we follow Him (Lk. xiv.33). What He then hands back to us is completely at His disposal; henceforth, we but hold it as stewards for Him; it is His to give or withhold at will" (pp. 162-63). It is easy for many to stand on the outside looking in when a question of wealth is raised. They feel that because they are not wealthy, biblical references to wealth do not apply to them. But often possessions or the desire for them have a greater grip on those with little than on those who have much. Right relationship to things is an issue that must be settled by all who will follow Christ.

After selling his possessions and giving to the poor, the rich young ruler was commanded to "follow" Jesus. Love of possessions was the obstacle to following but sale of them would not gain eternal life; identification with Christ would. At Christ's command, the man's face fell and he went away sad. It is common to assume that that was the end of the matter, but we do not know that it was. The inner struggle may have been long and severe. And it is not wrong to speculate that this man may have been one of those who sold his goods and contributed the proceeds to the common treasury of the early church after Pentecost (Acts 2:45).

The peril of riches (10:23-27). The rich young ruler had departed. Jesus "looked around" at the disciples to see what impression the incident had made on them. Then He proceeded to apply the lesson. "How difficult it is for those having riches to enter the kingdom of God!" Possessions occupy first place in one's life and get in the way of submitting to the rule of Christ. "The disciples were utterly astonished at his words." This concept cut across all contemporary Judaistic thinking. After all, hadn't the Old Testament taught that wealth and substance were marks of God's favor? And it was commonly taught that the rich accumulated merit through their good works. Then Jesus went on to say, "Little children," immature ones in the faith and in need of teaching, "how difficult it is for those who are leaning on their wealth to enter the kingdom of God." The danger for the rich lies in the temptation to trust in material resources rather than in God. They feel secure in their possessions and have little tendency to turn to God. "It is easier for a camel to go through a needle's eye," a contrast between the largest animal in Palestine and one of the smallest openings, is to be taken literally as an indication of impossibility. The needle's eye was found in a sewing needle and is not to be applied to a small passenger gate in a city wall, called a needle's eye since late medieval times.

Verse 25 must be linked to verse 24. Certainly the idea is that it is impossible for a rich person trusting in his riches to enter the kingdom; he must trust in the grace of God. "The disciples were even more amazed, and said to each other, 'Who then can be saved?'" (v. 26, NIV). "Amazed" here indicates indignation, despair, and bewilderment. The question of the disciples may also be translated "Who then will be found in the kingdom?" If the rich won't make it into the kingdom, who will? Jesus' answer in verse 27 in effect says, "Man may not have the power to get himself saved, but God has the power to effect deliverance, to bestow salvation."

The rewards of discipleship (10:28-31). Suddenly it flashed through

Peter's mind that he and the other disciples had met the requirements of discipleship enunciated to the rich young ruler. As spokesman for the group he expressed the fact to Jesus. "WE," (emphatic) for our part as contrasted with the rich young ruler, "have left" (aorist) in a complete break with the past, and "have followed" (perfect tense) from that day until now. According to Matthew 19:27 Peter then asked what their reward for service would be. Jesus' response is not a rebuke for Peter but a promise of reward for discipleship. Rewards will extend to all ("no man that hath left . . . but he shall receive"), will be at the optimum level of return ("hundredfold"), will be bestowed in the present age ("this time") and will include eternal life "in the age to come." But rewards will be accompanied by persecution, and will be of a sort different from the loss; e.g., loss of family will be compensated for by a new spiritual family (cf. Mark 3:31-35). Categories of loss include home, relatives, or property; and the goal of sacrifice is "for my sake, and the gospel's"—for the Lord and that the gospel of the Lord may be spread. It is hard to know whether verse 31 is meant to be a warning against the self-seeking spirit evident in verse 28 or whether it is an indication of reversal of earthly rank in the age to come.

The third passion announcement (10:32-34). The air is full of foreboding. From John's Gospel (chap. 11) it is clear that the raising of Lazarus had brought opposition to Jesus to a high level of intensity. Now Jesus is resolutely leading the way back to Jerusalem. As was customary for a rabbi or teacher, He went on ahead. Behind Him were the disciples "amazed" or "astonished" (same word as in v. 24), and behind them another group of followers who were "afraid." The tension of the moment arose either from something in the Lord's manner or from a vague sense of foreboding. As they were walking along Jesus took the Twelve aside and gave them the third passion announcement (cf. 8:31; 9:31). The new information here is that the suffering of Jesus will take place in Jerusalem, that not only would Israel reject her Messiah but would betray Him into the hands of the Gentiles, and that the Romans would then mock, spit upon, scourge, and kill Him. Here as before there appears vindication through resurrection.

Second discourse on greatness (10:35-45). Just as after the second passion announcement (9:30-32) a question had arisen among the disciples as to who was greatest among them (9:33-37), so after the third announcement the question arose again. It seems almost inconceivable that in the context of the announcement of the intense suffering of the

Master and in connection with all the emphasis on discipleship, becoming as children, and the like, that they should now be arguing about a leadership position in the kingdom. But there was a certain spiritual blindness that afflicted the disciples and their concept of a messianic kingdom was purely political. It was only natural that they should think about their role in that kingdom. At a distance of 2000 years and several thousand miles it is easy for us to judge them. Moreover, it is a certain evidence of faith that James and John should raise this question. They somehow have the confidence to believe the kingdom is to be set up, in spite of all the opposition to Jesus and His own predictions of suffering. As an added note, Salome, mother of James and John, was the instigator of the project and was ambitious for her sons (Matt. 20:20-21). If Salome was the sister of the Virgin Mary, as is commonly thought (but not proved), then there was reason why her sons (cousins of Jesus) should have special prominence in the kingdom.

James and John approached Jesus (v. 35) as one would approach a ruling sovereign, seeking a monarch's boon. But Jesus declined to assume this royal role and asked that they state their request. Their desire to sit on the right and left of Jesus in the kingdom is, of course, a desire to enjoy the chief places of honor in the kingdom. Jesus replied, "You do not know what you ask for yourselves." They spoke in ignorance, not knowing that suffering rather than glory lay ahead. Then Jesus asked, "Are you able to drink the cup I myself am drinking" (active, voluntary), "or be baptized with the baptism with which I am being baptized?" (passive, no doubt a baptism of blood or an immersion in suffering). Again they rushed to speak out of ignorance, "We are able." They committed themselves in a burst of loyalty. Without trying to impart understanding to two who were incapable of taking in the significance of what was going on at the moment, Jesus simply informed them that they would indeed drink the cup and suffer the baptism. As a matter of fact, James became the first apostle to suffer martyrdom (Acts 12:2) and late in life John was exiled to the Isle of Patmos where he received the vision of the Revelation. Positions in the kingdom were not His to give but would be appointed by the Father (cf. Matt. 20:23).

Evidently Salome, James, and John had made the request just discussed. Soon the rest of the disciples came into the picture and learned about what was going on. They were indignant at the two, perhaps for trying to "beat them out." At any rate, Jesus used a divisive situation as a teaching opportunity. Those who rule the Gentiles, who adhere to the worldly principle of greatness, "exercise lordship" from above. "But" among members of the kingdom the principle is reversed. "The one who wishes to become great among you shall be your ministrant" (*diakonos*, from which we get deacon). "The one who wants to be first among you shall be slave [*doulos*] of all." The one who wants to be first takes the lowest position of all, the position of slave, giving up his rights to serve others. "Preeminence in Christ's kingdom is attained through primacy in self-sacrificing services voluntarily rendered" (Hiebert, p. 261).

The messianic King Himself is the most illustrious example of the principle just enunciated (v. 45, commonly regarded as the key verse in the book). "For the Son of man," God's incarnate Son, voluntarily "came, not to be ministered unto," not to lord it over others, "but to minister," to give Himself in serving others, "and to give [voluntarily] his life a ransom [price paid to win release of one held in bondage] in place of many."

Blind Bartimaeus (10:46-52). As Jesus and His disciples crossed the Jordan and traveled toward Jerusalem, they took the usual route through Jericho. Along the way a crowd of Passover pilgrims joined them. At Jericho the healing of blind Bartimaeus occurred. It is fitting to report this miracle here because it illustrates again the Son of man's ministering, and because Bartimaeus shows some recognition of Jesus' messiahship (calling Him "Son of David"). This is significant as He heads toward the cross.

When this account is placed alongside that of Matthew and Luke, differences occur which critics have sought to use to prove contradictions in the Bible. Especially noteworthy is the fact that Mark and Matthew report the miracle took place as Jesus was going out of Jericho and Luke as He was drawing near it. Mark and Luke mention one blind man, while Matthew says there were two. At least three suggestions have been made for reconciling the geographical difference. First, in Jesus' day there were two Jerichos. One was a small village at the site of Old Testament Jericho and the other was New Testament Jericho, one to two miles south of it. The miracle took place between the two. Mark and Matthew view it as occurring on Jesus' way out of the one, while Luke thinks of it as happening on the way into the other. Second, the Lukan passage may be rendered "being near to Jericho" (Luke 18:35) without reference to whether He was coming out or going in. Third, what actually happened was that Jesus passed through Jericho, evidently the New Testament town, and received no invitation to spend the night. On the other side of town He met Zacchaeus and then returned with him to spend the night at the publican's house. As they returned to Jericho the healing took place. It occurred, then, after Jesus had passed through Jericho but on His way back into town. As to the number of persons involved, Mark and Luke concentrate on the vocal member of the pair, while Matthew gives the fuller account.

"Bartimaeus" and "son of Timaeus" say the same thing; "bar" is the Aramaic for "son." So "Bartimaeus" is Aramaic and "son of Timaeus" an explanatory word for Greco-Roman readers. As the two blind men saw the crowd going by they inquired about the commotion and were told that Jesus of Nazareth passed by. Then they began to yell with all their might, "Son of David, Jesus, show me mercy." Many tried to silence them, for what reason is not clear. Perhaps the suggestion that they simply did not want to be bothered is as good as any. Beggars of one sort or another were a common sight and a nuisance to those more fortunate. But Jesus chose to notice the pleas and to accept an ascription of messiahship before the whole crowd. Only once before, to the woman at the well in Samaria (John 4), had Jesus revealed Himself as Messiah, and that privately. Now, just before the crucifixion, it is time to do so publicly. Jesus gave the order, "Call him." Those who obeyed said, "Cheer up! Get up! He is calling you!" With all possible speed the suppliant came.

Then Jesus made him repeat publicly what it was he wanted. Of course Jesus knew what the beggar wanted. The whole crowd knew it. But vocalizing the request made it specific and constituted a confession of faith in Jesus and His ability to heal.

So it must often be with us. God knows our needs; many of our friends do too. But expressing them not only makes them specific but in a public prayer meeting involves a testimony to the power and glory of God. "Rabboni," my lord, my master, "let me receive my sight." Bartimaeus had recognized Jesus as the Messiah and now as lord. His whole demeanor was that he believed Jesus could restore his sight. Jesus' response, "your faith has saved you," must in this case have both a physical and spiritual reference. "Immediately he received his sight" and followed Jesus "on the road" and (according to Luke) both he and the crowd continued to give praise to God.

For Further Study

1. Compare Jesus' attention to children in chapters 9 and 10.

2. Note and comment on the attitudes toward Jesus displayed in Mark 9:30–10:52.

3. What evidence is there for more need of training on the part of the disciples in Mark 9:30–10:52?

4. Compare the three passion announcements.

5. Compare the healings of the blind in chapters 8 and 10.

6. What titles for Jesus appear in chapter 10? What do they signify?

Chapter 13

Jesus' Kingly Authority
(Mark 11:1-26)

Jesus' kingly authority is evident in this chapter in His triumphal entry into Jerusalem, His cleansing of the temple, and His cursing of the fig tree and its sudden withering.

Triumphal entry into Jerusalem (11:1-11). The week had finally arrived for which Jesus had been born—the week in which He would bear the penalty of sin for the entire human race. He would begin the week with an assertion of messiahship and the triumphal entry into Jerusalem, and end it as the resurrected Lord of glory. The Gospel of John (12:1, 12-15) makes it clear that the triumphal entry occurred on the Sunday before Easter. John also supplies the information that Jesus spent Saturday at Bethany and that popular fervor had been whipped up by the raising of Lazarus. Bethany, the home of Mary, Martha, and Lazarus, and Jesus' headquarters during the first part of Passion week, was and is about two miles east of Jerusalem on the eastern slope of the Mount of Olives. Bethphage has completely disappeared but it is thought to have been on the western slope of the mount. Incidentally, the Mount of Olives rises to about 2,680 feet above sea level and is separated from Jerusalem by the Kidron Valley.

After Jesus and the disciples had left Bethany and were near Bethphage (see Matt. 21:1), Jesus sent two of the disciples into Bethphage with specific instructions. Who the two were is not known but it usually assumed that Peter was one of them because Mark, who wrote under the influence of Peter, includes so many eyewitness details. It is not necessary to conclude that the provision of the colt for Jesus to ride was merely a result of divine omniscience. Possibly Jesus had made arrangements with the owner. It seems clear that as Jesus prepared to ride into Jerusalem He intended to fulfill the messianic prophecy of Zechariah 9:9, but He did not make a point of the matter with the disciples or the crowds. Unused animals were regarded as especially suited for sacred purposes. Although arrangements to use the colt may not have been a result of foreknowledge, specific detail about conditions the two disciples would face certainly were. If anyone tries to stop you, simply say, "The Lord needs it and will send it back here shortly" (NIV), was Jesus' instruction. Almost certainly questioners would have had to know Jesus and the disciples well to have accepted such an answer. Jesus is careful to make clear that He wants to borrow the animal only for a little while.

The disciples carried out their instructions to the letter. They found the colt tied at the owner's door in the open street with its mother and were given permission by the owner (Luke 19:33) to bring them both (Matt. 21:2). According to the Matthew passage Jesus wanted the mother to accompany the colt, evidently so the young animal would behave in docile fashion. Of course the colt had no saddle; so the disciples threw their outer robes on its back. Then the disciples set Jesus on the colt (Luke 19:35) and He rode toward the city. Behind Him and around Him was a crowd of people who evidently had gathered in Bethany to see Lazarus and Jesus. Now they began to *pave* the dusty road before Jesus with their outer robes, branches of trees, leaves, straw, and other litter "cut from the fields." This action may be viewed as a kind of royal salute or a gesture of respect, as that given to Jehu (2 Kings 9:12ff.) or Simon the Hasmonean (1 Macc. 13:51).

Apparently long before this, word had spread in Jerusalem that Jesus had left Bethany and was on the way to the Holy City. So a second crowd went forth from the city carrying palm branches (John 12:12-13). Evidently the two groups met on the slope of the Mount of Olives (Luke 19:37) and at that point began the chant recorded in Mark 11:9-10 and parallel passages in the other three Gospels. The words "Blessed is he that cometh in the name of the LORD" were from Psalm 118:26 and were part of the Hallel sung especially at Passover. From the parallel passages it is clear that the crowd also hailed Him as Son of David and King of Israel. "Hosanna" originally was a prayer meaning "Save, we pray," but came to signify simply "Hail." Evidently this triumphal procession was some sort of messianic recognition, but one must not push understanding of it too far. When asked to identify Jesus, the crowd itself said on reaching Jerusalem, "This is Jesus the prophet of Nazareth of Galilee."

And John 12:16 records: "These things understood not his disciples."

At any rate, after the two crowds met they escorted Jesus into Jerusalem, where the inhabitants were profoundly stirred by the event (Matt. 21:10). And the Pharisees were worried because it appeared "the world is gone after him" (John 12:19). But there is no evidence that the Romans thought the procession and demonstration to be anything more than a religious event related to the Passover season. Evidently the crowd broke up soon after reaching the city and apparently Jesus was accompanied by only the Twelve as He made His inspection tour of the temple (Mark 11:11). From what follows, Jesus must have been deeply disturbed by what He saw there; but the hour was late and efforts to rectify the situation would have to wait until the next day. The apostolic company went out to Bethany for the night.

Cursing the fig tree (11:12-14). On Monday morning as Jesus and the disciples came over the Mount of Olives on their way to Bethany, He became hungry. Why, is not explained. Certainly Mary and Martha would not have sent Him away without breakfast, and He could not have been much more than a mile or so from their house. Perhaps He was too engrossed in the concerns of the day to eat. In His state of hunger He came upon a solitary fig tree along the road and found nothing on it but leaves. So He cursed it to the effect that it would never bear fruit again.

As a matter of fact, Jesus did not expect to find on the tree any figs He could eat, "for it was not the season for figs." He did, however, expect to see some evidence of fruit. Normally figs came before leaves or at least by the time the leaves did. So here was a profession of fruitfulness but no real fruit. The judgment on the tree must be interpreted as an act of symbolic judgment similar to that of some of the Old Testament prophets. In the Old Testament Israel often is likened to a fig tree and the destruction of a fig tree likened to judgment (see, e.g., Hos. 2:12; 9:10,16; Mic. 7:1-6; Jer. 8:13; 29:17). Embedded in the fig tree narrative (see vv. 20-25) is judgment on the spiritually unproductive group in the temple. As Lane observes, "Just as the leaves of the tree concealed the fact that there was no fruit to enjoy, so the magnificence of the Temple and its ceremony conceals the fact that Israel has not brought forth the fruit of righteousness demanded by God" (p. 400). Incidentally, this was a free-standing tree along the road, belonging to no one; Jesus cannot be accused of destroying private property.

Cleansing the temple (11:15-19). Worshipers who came to the temple from a distance had to buy sacrificial animals and birds locally.

Moreover, those who came from many lands had to get their currency changed into the sacred shekel so they could pay their temple tax. The "sons of Annas," including Caiaphas, the reigning high priest, had established booths for money changers and the sale of birds and animals in the court of the Gentiles in the temple. All the noise and confusion prevented the Gentiles from having a house of prayer. Worse, the family of Annas evidently was charging unreasonable prices for sacrificial animals and birds and for changing money. A kind of religious mafia was siphoning off a considerable profit from the temple activities. There is no way of knowing whether Jesus was opposed to all economic activity in the temple or whether He was particularly incensed over the racket that the priesthood had going. In any case, He tossed out all this activity from the court of the Gentiles. Evidently this is the second cleansing of the temple, the first one occurring at the beginning of Jesus' public ministry (John 2:13-22).

It is doubtful that Jesus' cleansing of the temple can be used to support the view of some that no business of any kind may be carried on in the church today. Probably at least two questions should be asked in dealing with such a matter: would the business contemplated in any way hinder the spiritual ministry of the church? Would it actually enhance the spiritual ministry of the church (e.g., a book table)?

The scriptural warrant for Jesus' cleansing of the temple (11:17) is found in Isaiah 56:7 and evidently involves a messianic claim. It is clear from verse 18 that Jesus' drastic action threatened not only the establishment itself but also its economic policies. And He had especially incurred the wrath of the temple authorities in connection with His concern for the spiritual welfare of the Gentiles. From this point on no effort is spared to destroy Him.

The withered fig tree (11:20-26). The next day as the disciples accompanied Jesus from Bethany to Jerusalem, they noticed the fig tree that He had cursed already withering away and were astonished at the suddenness of the death of the tree—in effect, at the evidence of Christ's power over nature (Matt. 21:19-22). Immediately Jesus called the disciples' attention to the source of the power demonstrated: "go on having complete reliance on God." He says, in effect, your faith in the power of God is limitless. A person could even tell the Mount of Olives to be removed over there into the Dead Sea and it would be done, but there must be no wavering in the belief that the request would be granted. In other words, faith must be absolute. Of course Jesus was not recommending silly prayers; He was talking about dealing with impossible situations. And though the concept is not interjected here, one cannot have absolute faith in the omnipotent power of God to accomplish something unless he has confidence that what he asks is in the will of God.

In verse 24 Jesus goes on to make the general principle just enunciated personal. In verse 23 it is "whoever shall say"; here it is "all things . . . you ask for." "Therefore . . . because of the power of faith united to the omnipotence of God" (Hiebert, p. 281), "all things . . . you go on asking for touching your affairs, go on believing that you did receive them [count the prayer already granted] and you shall have them." But verse 25 introduces an important condition: if we have an unforgiving spirit against others, we cannot expect God to forgive us or to hear us. As Cole observes, "We have no inherent right to be heard by God. . . unless we forgive our fellow man freely, it shows that we have no consciousness of the grace that we ourselves have received . . . and thus that we are expecting to be heard on our own merits" (p. 181). Verse 26 is not in the best manuscripts and should be omitted here. It is generally thought to be an insertion from Matthew 6:15, where it is certainly genuine.

For Further Study

1. What attitudes toward Jesus can you find in this chapter?
2. What does Jesus teach about prayer in this chapter?
3. What information about the Twelve do you glean from this chapter?
4. What is the meaning of the triumphal entry to Jesus? to the Twelve? to the multitude? to us?

Chapter 14

Temple Cross-examination
(Mark 11:27 – 12:44)

The time is Tuesday of Passion Week. The place is the temple. Yesterday Jesus launched a frontal attack on the entrenched forces of the priesthood there. Today we find Him walking in the temple (11:27ff.), teaching in the temple (12:35ff.), and sitting in the temple (12:41ff.). While He is there, opposition to Him heightens: chief priests, scribes, elders (the three elements of the Sanhedrin), Pharisees, Herodians, and Sadducees all seek to trip Him up with a variety of questions. But He is equal to the task and effectively cross-examines or counterattacks, and the section ends with Jesus in complete control. From this time on Jesus' enemies apparently recognize that it will be impossible to outwit Him. Henceforth, they will take the route of plot, force, misrepresentation, and political pressure to destroy Jesus.

The question of authority (11:27-33). After Jesus' discussion with the disciples about the withered fig tree and faith and prayer, the group had come to the temple area where Jesus proceeded to teach (Luke 20:1). Members of the council of the Jews, the Sanhedrin (chief priests, scribes, elders), waited until He finished His discourse and then posed a question, "By what authority are you doing these things?" This they quickly followed by another, "Who gave you this authority so that you are doing these things?" That is, what kind of authority do You possess and who gave it to You? "These things," is deliberately vague and would include the teaching He had just concluded, the cleansing of the temple the previous day, and other aspects of His ministry. The Sanhedrin were hardly seeking information. They knew what authority Jesus claimed and were not about to accept it, for to do so would be tantamount to accepting Him as Messiah. Their aim now was to get Him to state His claims and then to deny Him His authority.

Jesus replied with a counter question, a common rabbinical method of reply. It should not be regarded as an evasion but an effort to put the question more squarely on target, an inquiry made for the sake of one's questioner. "John's baptism—was it from heaven, or from men?" (v. 30, NIV). "So the Lord, instead of a direct answer, virtually tells them that His authority stems from the same source as that of John the Baptist" (Cole, p. 182). And they are caught on the horns of a dilemma. If John's mission had a heavenly origin, they should have believed him; if it was of human origin, they would have made him an imposter and he would have been in danger of the excitable Passover crowds. By this time, no doubt numerous people were listening to the interrogation. It would not have been safe for the Sanhedrin to deny the power of God upon John. They were not concerned with true answers but safe answers. They decided to plead ignorance, "We don't know"—and to look ridiculous. The Lord responded to such deliberate ignorance by pleading ignorance to the question they had asked Him. As Cole observed, "The Lord's question was not a trap; it was yet another opportunity for them to realize and confess their blindness, and ask for light. Theirs was the unforgivable sin" (p. 183).

The Parable of the Vineyard (12:1-12). Having silenced the Sanhedrin, Jesus was not through with them yet. He had a further message for them, a message of doom, in the parable of the vineyard, otherwise called the parable of the wicked husbandmen or the parable of the rejection of the Son. "Jesus began to speak to them in parables" (v. 1), but Mark records only one. Matthew (21–22) relates three; how many there were we do not know. Here a great and wealthy man (God) plants a vineyard (Israel) leaving out nothing in its proper establishment. Then He leased it to vine-growers (rulers of Israel) and went off a considerable distance. The tenant farmers were expected to pay a certain percentage of the crop to the landlord at each harvest. At the background of this parable is Isaiah 5; there all Israel was guilty before God for their failure; here the rulers of Israel are guilty.

Periodically the owner sent out slaves (prophets) to receive His share of the crop. Instead of fruits of contrition and trust, the keepers of the vineyard roughly handled the slaves. One (v. 3) they beat up and sent away empty-handed, a second they wounded in the head and dishonored and insulted, a third they killed. As time went on the owner sent many others to collect his due, with the same result of beatings and killings. The patience of God did not wear thin; He continued to send His servants. Finally, the owner had only one left to send, "a beloved son," whom He sent "last of all" as an ultimate appeal to the vine-growers. But they plotted among themselves to kill him so they could claim the inheritance.

The reference is clear; the Jewish leaders found Jesus to be an obstacle to their control over Israel and they were determined to kill Him so they could preserve their hold on the Jews. In fact, this very Sanhedrin whom Jesus was addressing had been plotting to kill Him ever since the raising of Lazarus (John 11:47-53). Cole aptly observes, "It was not through their failure to recognize the Son that they killed Him; that would have been pardonable. It was, as in the parable, precisely because they recognized Him for who He was that they slew Him. . . . We reject the claims of Christ not because we misunderstand them, but because we understand them only too well, in spite of all our protestations to the contrary" (p. 185).

At this juncture Jesus evidently addressed a question to the crowd, "What then will the owner of the vineyard do?" (v. 9, NIV). As is clear from Matthew 21:41, the crowd responded with the judgment that the owner would kill the vinedressers and give the vineyard to others. Jesus accepted this verdict and went on to quote a confirming prophecy from Psalm 118:22-23. The application is clear: "The stone [Christ] which the builders [the Jewish leaders involved in constructing the old order] rejected [because it did not pass their tests] has now become the corner head [binding together two adjoining walls in a whole new structure (church or New Covenant)]. This [wonderful arrangement, or exaltation of Christ] is the Lord's doing." The Sanhedrin "wanted to grab Him [Jesus], because they knew His story was aimed at them, but they were afraid of the crowd" (v. 12, Beck), and they did not want to appear to understand the parable. So they simply slunk off.

Question concerning tribute (12:13-17). Having been so thoroughly discredited by Jesus, the Sanhedrin wasted no time in launching a further attack on Him. "They sent some of the Pharisees and Herodians to him." Such strange bedfellows! The Pharisees hated any foreign domination and of course opposed paying taxes to a foreign power, though they did so; the Herodians, supporters of Rome would favor such payment of taxes. So great was their dislike of Jesus that the two teamed up, as they did in Galilee (see Mark 3:6), to see if they could "snare" (a word used of a hunter stalking his prey) Jesus with some question. The question they raised concerned whether or not tribute should be paid to Caesar. If He said yes He would alienate the Pharisees and the Jews generally; if He said no, He would offend the Herodians and invite reprisals from Roman authorities. Their approach to Jesus was to bear witness to His integrity and His fearless devotion to the truth of God, paying no attention to the opinions of men. This statement (vv. 14-15a) was not mere palaver; it was designed to force Him to face the issue they were about to raise, in a nonevasive way.

Jesus was not only clever, He was omniscient and saw through their facade immediately. "Why are you putting me to the test," He asked, letting them know He saw what they were up to. Then Jesus told them to bring Him a denarius, the coin with which the poll tax was always paid. This silver coin was the normal wage of a day laborer. Jesus then asked whose image and whose inscription were on the coin, and they answered "Caesar's." This Caesar would have been Tiberius (who ruled A.D. 14-37) and the inscription would have claimed that he was the son of the divine Augustus and hence semidivine himself. Then Jesus responded, "Give to Caesar what is Caesar's and to God what is God's" (v. 17, NIV). In effect this statement said that Caesar had the right to mint coins, levy taxes, and govern, and these did not infringe on the rights of God. His listeners also had obligations to God. Jesus' sharp distinction between the two spheres implied rejection of the idea that Caesar was divine, but it did not imply any necessary conflict between the two areas of responsibility. The basic principles were there but people have argued about the precise relationship of the two spheres ever since. Again Jesus had silenced His questioners. "They were utterly dumbfounded at Him" (Williams).

Question concerning the resurrection (12:18-27). Now the Sadducees tried their hand at discrediting Jesus. Of the priestly establishment, they would feel as threatened as the Pharisees by the successes of Jesus and the possibility that He might set up His kingdom. Influenced by the nonsupernaturalism of Greco-Roman thought, they did not believe in the resurrection of the body, the immortality of the soul, or the existence of angels and spirits. But they were firm adherents to the law of Moses. On this occasion they decided to raise the question about the Resurrection and tried to make the concept look ridiculous by treating it in the most literal way. Verse 19 is a brief statement of the principle of Levirate marriage (marrying the childless wife of a dead brother, in order to prevent his line from dying out, cf. Deut. 25:5-10). The Sadducees erected a straw man by dragging out the principle to apply to all seven brothers and then asking whose wife she would be in the Resurrection. Conceivably the story was adapted from the apocryphal book Tobit, which mentions a woman married to seven husbands, all of whom died childless (Tobit 3:8).

In His reply Jesus first stigmatizes the Sadducees for failure to understand either the tenor of the Scripture or the power of God. If they properly understood the power of God, they would not have doubted His power to raise the dead. They would see this problem in a larger context of the whole spiritual world of which angels (which they reject) are a part. Marriage ceases to have any sexual importance in heaven and the resurrection life of men and women will be like that of the angels: it will center on communion with God.

Next, in verses 26, 27, Jesus proceeds to deal with the Sadducees' failure to understand the tenor of Scripture. He reminds them of Moses' experience at the burning bush when God told Moses, "I am the God of Abraham, the God of Isaac, and the God of Jacob." And Jesus concludes, "He is not the God of the dead, but the God of the living." In other words, for God to say to Moses centuries after the death of the patriarchs, "I am the God of . . . ," requires that this fact is still true, that the patriarchs are still alive in the invisible world. "He is the *God of the living* because He is the living God Himself; and so too Christ could describe Himself as 'the life' (Jn. xi. 25) . . . even in the physical realm, contact with Him brought new life to the dead (cf. Mk. v.41); thus to know God, and the Christ whom He sent, is itself life eternal (Jn. xvii.3)" (Cole, p. 191). As a parting thrust Jesus says to the Sadducees, "You are greatly deceiving yourselves" in denying the Resurrection.

Question concerning the greatest commandment (12:28-34). Matthew draws aside the curtain to give some preparation for the next episode: "Hearing that Jesus had silenced the Sadducees, the Pharisees got together. One of them . . . tested him" (22:34-35, NIV). The Pharisees, supernaturalists of the day, would have been pleased with Jesus' defense of the Resurrection and related questions about life after death. They chose one of their number, "an expert in the law," to present their question about the law to test Jesus' skill in dealing with the law. There is no apparent malice in this conversation; the lawyer was straightforward in his approach and Jesus commended him for his answer and attitude. The Pharisees spent a lot of time debating about the law, from which they had deduced 613 individual statutes, and there was a concern among them to determine which were the weightiest of the lot. So this lawyer or scribe, who had stood by during the earlier contest with the Sadducees, now put his question, "What kind of commandment is first of all," i.e., was to be ranked in highest place?

Jesus met His listener on his own ground, at his own stage of development and then sought to lead him on. As a pious Jew he would have recited in worship that morning the Shema (Deut. 6:4-9; 11:13-21; Num. 15:37-41) as a kind of confession. Jesus quoted to him Deuteronomy 6:4-5 (Mark 12:29,30). The Lord, the great unique absolute being of the universe, is "our God"; we are the object of His covenant love. From this distinctive relationship to Him flows the duty to love Him with a love that flows out of every area of one's being: heart, soul, mind, strength. "Clearly this cannot be the subject of legal enactment. It is a matter of will and action. The love which determines the whole disposition of one's life and places one's whole personality in the service of God reflects commitment to God which springs from divine sonship" (Lane, pp. 432-3).

The second commandment, "like" the first (Matt. 22:39) in nature, is "You shall love your neighbor as yourself" (Lev. 19:18). While the neighbor for the Jew meant "the children of thy people" (Lev. 19:18), Jesus broadened that concept considerably in the Parable of the Good Samaritan (Luke 10:25-37). Love for another involves many things, among which are respect, consideration, acceptance, desire for his success, and giving one's self to him. The assumption here seems to be that one has love for self and is now exhorted to love his neighbor as himself. But on the basis of many years of teaching and counseling, the writer would like to suggest that one reason why many today do not love others any more than they do is that they really do not love themselves. They may be self-centered, but that is not the same as loving one's self. This question deserves much more thought.

The lawyer bestows a transparent commendation on Jesus for His reply. And in his rehearsal of Jesus' answer he significantly adds that proper heart attitude toward God and others was more important than meticulous adherence to the ceremonial aspects of Judaism and the bringing of sacrifices, though of course he was not repudiating all that. In verse 34, Jesus offers a commendation of His own. He saw that the scribe answered "intelligently"; "The idea is that he in all sincerity grasped what Jesus had told him" (Lenski, p. 542). Moreover, Jesus told him that he was "not far from the kingdom." To get closer and to enter that kingdom, the scribe would have to recognize his own inadequacy in loving God and his neighbor and to throw himself on God's love and grace for forgiveness. "From that point on no one dared ask him any more questions." All their efforts to bring Him into disrepute with political authorities, to compromise His orthodoxy, or to entangle Him in inconsistencies or ill-advised statements of His own position had come to naught.

Paradoxical question about David's Son (12:35-37). But while a group of scribes is still before Him, Jesus poses a question of biblical understanding of His own. During the Passover season there was heightened hope of the coming of Messiah. In fact, on Sunday the throngs had made some messianic statements about Jesus. And on the basis of the Old Testament, Judaism generally accepted the idea that the Messiah would be a son of David. Now Jesus asks, "What do the scribes mean when they say that Christ is the son of David?" He observed that David himself (assuming that David wrote Ps. 110:1) by inspiration of the Holy Spirit said: "The Lord said to my Lord: Sit at my right hand until I put your enemies under your feet," (v. 36, NIV). "The Lord," Yahweh or Jehovah, said to "my Lord," Adonai. Clearly both persons referred to are members of the Godhead. The place at "my right hand" is the place of honor in heaven itself; and enthronement there would continue for an indefinite time, until Christ returns to sit on the throne of David on earth. "David calls him Lord; so how is he then his son?" How can Messiah be David's son if David calls Him Lord? The scribes recognized Messiah would be the son of David, but Jesus shows that Messiah must be regarded as more than a man.

"The masses kept on hearing him with delight" are words which probably indicate the enthusiastic response of the temple crowds or bystanders to His handling of the various groups who came to Him. These words do not necessarily indicate, however, that they understood or appropriated the truths He enunciated.

Condemnation of the Scribes (12:38-40). Having shown the inability of the scribes as interpreters of Scripture, Jesus went on to condemn the scribes and Pharisees themselves (Matt. 23:1-2). "In his teaching he was saying," indicates Mark is here reporting snatches of things Jesus said about the scribes and Pharisees (see a longer version in Matt. 23). And certainly what is said does not apply to all of them; some, like the one appearing earlier in this chapter, were seeking after God, and many of them came to receive the Messiah. "Beware of the scribes," be on guard against their evil influence, He warns. Then in general terms He condemns categories of behavior among them: (1) their personal appearance and ostentation—they wore long, white-fringed robes that distinguished them in any crowd and won them deference bordering on worship when they circulated in public; (2) their social and ecclesiastical relationships—they sought chief places at feasts and chief seats in synagogues; (3) their financial dealings—they took advantage of people of limited means (devoured widows' houses); (4) their personal devotional life—their pretext of deep piety with long public prayers. This denunciation of scribal practices concludes Jesus' public ministry. The incident which follows, the Olivet Discourse (chap. 13) and the upper-room ministry were all directed toward the disciples.

The widow's mites (12:41-44). This brief account provides a sharp contrast to the sham righteousness of the scribes and Pharisees who wanted all they could get from society. Here is a woman whose total devotion to God led her to give all she had. Jesus and the disciples had left the temple area proper and had entered the Court of the Women. The treasury or offering chests were located there so the women could have access to them. Thirteen trumpet-shaped receptacles for offerings were placed against the wall of the Court of the Women and were marked with purposes for which the contributions would be used.

Jesus sat and watched people coming to make their offerings. The crowds were large because it was Passover season, and many brought substantial gifts. Finally a destitute widow gave two "mites," or *lepta,* the smallest copper coin in circulation in Palestine, which Mark (for the benefit of Roman readers) said were equal to one *quadrans,* a Roman copper coin. This equation helps to support the assertion that Mark was writing in the West because the *quadrans* was not in circulation in the East. The value of the *lepton* or *quadrans* cannot be translated meaningfully into contemporary currency, except to say that the *quadrans* was one sixty-fourth of a *denarius,* a laborer's daily wage. But of course the important thing is not what the gift was worth; it was absolutely *all the woman had.* Probably she would have to fast until she could find a way to earn more. Jesus used the example of the sacrificial gift of the widow to teach the disciples a lesson: what matters most in the sight of God is not the size of the gift but the degree of commitment to God and the amount of sacrifice it represents.

For Further Study

1. Study the major questions asked in this section. How do they differ as to motivation? How are they consistent with the questioner? What was Jesus' method of handling the question? Was it the same in each case?

2. What use does Mark make of the Old Testament in this section?

3. What can be learned about the doctrine of God from this section?

4. What attitudes toward Jesus appear in this section?

Chapter 15

The Olivet Discourse
(Mark 13:1-37)

As the golden rays of the setting sun flooded the magnificent temple of Herod, Jesus and His disciples sat opposite this center of Judaism on the western slope of the Mount of Olives. The words Jesus uttered on that Tuesday evening of Passion Week are capsulized in Mark 13 and Luke 21 but appear more at length in Matthew 24 - 25. Since Jesus spoke these words on the Mount of Olives, they are commonly called the Olivet Discourse. While it is a prophecy concerning the future, it is also something of a farewell address to the disciples and provides warning and encouragement to faith and obedience. Moreover, it furnishes a bridge between Jesus' ministry and the Passion narrative. As Lane notes, "By locating the eschatological discourse in this crucial position, and by recurring reference to the destruction of the Temple in the context of Jesus' trial and execution (Chs. 14:58; 15:29, 39), the evangelist points to the relationship which exists between the judgment upon Jerusalem implied by the discourse and the death of Jesus" (p. 444).

The occasion (13:1-4). As Jesus and the disciples left the temple area, one of the disciples remarked to Him about what a marvelous structure it was. A complex of courts, porches, and buildings, it covered about one-sixth of the city of Jerusalem. Jesus' reply was the startling prediction that it would be completely dismantled—"not one stone shall be left upon another." Then there is no further recorded conversation for perhaps a half hour. It is possible everyone was too stunned to speak. Finally, as Jesus sat on the Mount of Olives opposite the temple, Peter, James, John, and Andrew decided to ask Him more about this tragic prediction. "Asked" is in the singular and probably Peter was the one who broached the subject. "Privately" probably means in the company of the Twelve alone when a larger group of followers was not present. So they asked a triple question according to Matthew 24:3: when these things would occur, what would be the sign of His coming, and of the end of the age. The rest of the chapter provides Jesus' answer.

The interpretation. In order to work out the interpretation of Mark 13 it is necessary to go to Matthew 24, where there is a little fuller account. And it will be useful to read the NASB of Matthew 24, where there is reference to "tribulation" in verse 9, "great tribulation" (v. 21) and "after the tribulation" (v. 29). Moreover, it is indispensable to consult Daniel 9:27 for the background of Mark 13:14 (cf. Matt. 24:15). Daniel states clearly that at the beginning of the Tribulation a prince will make a covenant with the Jews; and in the middle of the week he will break that covenant, will cause sacrifices to cease, and will cause an abomination of desolation to occur. What is clear from both Matthew 24:15 and Mark 13:14 is that the abomination of desolation (evidently some pagan altar or image) is then introduced and great tribulation or the last half of the Tribulation then occurs. It is also clear from both Matthew 24:29 and Mark 13:24 that at the end of the great Tribulation Christ will return. Furthermore, if Matthew 24:15 and Mark 13:14 mark the middle of the Tribulation, then part of what precedes must have something to do with the first half of the Tribulation. Matthew 24:9 (NASB) says, "They will deliver you up to tribulation" and verse 8 talks about the "beginning of pains" or "sorrows"; Mark 13:8 also talks about the "beginnings of sorrows."

It is not clear whether the beginning of the first half of the Tribulation is to be set at verse 8 or 9 or whether some of what appears in previous verses is also to be considered as part of the Tribulation. So apparently what we have in Mark 13:5ff. is some reference to conditions in the disciples' own day and possibly in centuries to follow, unless Jesus meant to start answering immediately in verse 5 the question of what would be the sign of the end of the age and of His coming. But at least by verse 8 we are probably dealing with conditions of the first half of the Tribulation, to be followed in verse 14 by events which introduce the great Tribulation or the last half of the Tribulation, and to be followed in verse 24 by the return of Christ. This is of course a posttribulation return of Christ in judgment and has nothing to do with the question of a pretribulation rapture, which is not in view in Mark 13 or Matthew 24 - 25. Therefore this complicated subject is not discussed here. It should be noted that Jesus addresses the disciples as representatives of the Jews in Mark 13. Though the earlier verses of the chapter may apply specifically to them, the latter ones cannot.

Earlier trials (13:5-13). In these verses Jesus warns against pretenders, catastrophic occurrences, and persecution. "Be vigilant that no one misleads you" (v. 5). "In my name" (v. 6) signifies "arrogating to themselves the title and authority which properly belong to me" (Lane, p. 457). Wars and rumors of wars, earthquakes, and famines have, of course, plagued the world ever since Jesus' sojourn on earth. But the intensity has grown in this century and will be much worse at the end time. The bombing of London, Berlin, Hiroshima, and Nagasaki, for example, show how terrible war can be and give some inkling of the terrors of the future. The terrible earthquakes of 1976 had even the press talking prophetically. The loss of a reported 750,000 people in the great Chinese quake dwarfed other tragedies in Guatemala (about 23,000 died), the Philippines (over 4,000 died), Italy, Indonesia, and elsewhere. The 1977 devastation of Bucharest, Romania, is another example of the continuing saga of earthquake tragedy. Famines also occur with increasing intensity, and worldwide famine has now become a distinct possibility.

Verses 9-13 predict persecution and constitute a call to steadfastness under persecution. Persecutions will be religious (beatings in Sanhedrins and synagogues), political (governors and kings), domestic and social (betrayed by relatives). Under such circumstances believers have every prop removed and are cast on God alone. Though persecutions, like other trials, have occurred in all ages, they will intensify during the Tribulation. But it is certainly true in all ages that those under trial may depend on the Holy Spirit for a proper word to speak.

Two appropriate illustrations of His help in the present age come to mind. A believer in Kenya during the Mau Mau troubles was about to be hacked to pieces. He happened to be wearing a white coat; and wishing to bear a testimony, he offered it to one of his captors with the word that it was a shame for it to be blood-spotted and ruined. The persecutors were not prepared for courage and graciousness like that and let him go. Second, a student of the writer at the Moody Bible Institute was engaged in some ministry in Chicago when a gang with brass knuckles accosted him and stood him up against a wall. Though he was too afraid to do anything, when they asked him why he did not act scared or fight or try to run away, the Lord gave him the words, "You can't touch me if

God won't let you." That was too much for them and they turned and walked away.

Two verses in this section require further comment: 10 and 13. Verse 10 talks about the necessity of preaching the gospel to all nations before the end time. The fuller statement appears in Matthew 24:14, "And this gospel of the kingdom shall be preached in the whole world for a witness to all the nations, and then shall the end come" (NASB). Gospel is "good news" and the good news about the coming kingdom and the imminent return of the king is not necessarily the same as the gospel of the grace of God. At any rate, whatever the content of the message, it is something that will be declared world-wide during the Tribulation and does not necessarily support the idea that if the church will hurry up and preach the gospel world-wide now it can hasten the Rapture. And, of course, world-wide preaching does not guarantee world-wide acceptance.

The promise in 13:13 that "he who endures to the end will be saved" has been used to confuse the condition for salvation. Clearly the basis of salvation in this present age is belief or faith in the finished work of Christ on the cross (more than 150 injunctions to belief appear in the New Testament). The appeal is not "believe and hold out" or some other such approach based on human effort. "The endurance, however, is not the basis of the salvation. In keeping with the general teaching of the NT, endurance is to be viewed as the result of the new birth (cf. Rom 8:28-29; I Jn 2:19)" (Burdick, p. 1016).

The Great Tribulation (13:14-23). The sign par excellence of the end of the age and of the coming of Christ (requested by the disciples), and the signal for the beginning of the great Tribulation is the abomination of desolation or "desolating sacrilege" (RSV). The "abomination" is an object that is detestable and in the Old Testament denoted idolatry or sacrilege (e.g., Deut. 29:16-17; 1 Kings 11:6-7). "Of desolation" indicates the effect produced: the "abomination that makes desolate." "Standing where he has no right to stand" (Williams) properly indicates that the participle "standing" is masculine.

Though Mark is indefinite as to the place where the abomination stands, Matthew 24:15 clearly states that it will be in the "holy place," requiring, of course, that the temple will be rebuilt before the second coming of Christ. It is interesting to note that the Antichrist or man of sin that Thessalonians describes as coming at the end times "takes his seat in the temple of God, proclaiming himself to be God" (2 Thess. 2:4, RSV).

The abomination of desolation is specifically connected with Daniel's prophecy of the seventieth week of years (the Tribulation, cf. Dan. 9:27) in Matthew 24:15 but not in the preferred text of Mark 13:14. In the middle of the Tribulation the prince, the political ruler, will break his covenant with the Jews, causing temple sacrifices to cease and the abomination of desolation to be set up. When that happens, Jesus said all will know that the great Tribulation has been launched.

Terrible persecution will descend on the Jews and extreme haste will be necessary to escape. One who is doing something on the flat top of his house when the news is flashed should not even go inside to pick up any belongings; he should flee by the outside stairway. One who is working in the field should not go to his house to get his outer cloak. Especially to be pitied are expectant and nursing mothers whose condition will impede flight. "Pray that it may not be in winter" when the rains fill the wadis[1] in the Judean hills and swell the streams and hinder movement. At that time will occur tribulation of unparalleled intensity, certainly the time of trial predicted in the Book of Revelation. In fact, it will be so severe that the population of the area would be wiped out if God "had not shortened," if He had not already decreed limits on the duration of the Tribulation. God set those limits for the sake of "the elect," true believers then living.

In the midst of all these trials false messiahs and false prophets will arise, no doubt promising to solve the problems or meet the needs of the hour. As credentials they will "show signs and wonders," either fabricating amazing things or by demonic activity actually performing miracles. The Revelation also predicts that demon-empowered persons will have miraculous power during the Tribulation (Rev. 13:13-15; 16:14; cf. 2 Thess. 2:9,10). So one should not conclude that all supernatural demonstrations prove that a ministry is of God. These false religious leaders will try to lead even true believers astray "if possible," but the inference is that such efforts will not be successful. "So be on your guard; I have told you everything ahead of time" (v. 23, NIV). I have told you everything you need to know to protect you from the evil one and to live effectively in the world. Often we want to know more about the future; but more knowledge of details would only satisfy our curiosity, it is not necessary to our effective functioning. They will know with assurance, however, whether or not a claimant is the Messiah, for the coming of the

---

[1]A wadi is a stream bed that is dry most of the year but may become a raging torrent during the rainy season.

Son of man will be "as lightning" (Matt. 24:27) and His coming will be accompanied by fearsome natural phenomena. In fact, when Messiah comes at the end of the Tribulation, everyone will know it.

Return of Messiah (13:24-27). After the great Tribulation, "immediately" after it (Matt. 24:29) shall appear a variety of cosmic disturbances which commentators commonly have treated as symbolizing political and international upheaval. But there is no reason why these predictions should not be taken literally. "Stars will be falling," one after the other, perhaps a hail of meteorites. "The powers in the heavens" may be a continuation of what has been said about the sun, moon, and stars and refer to physical forces of nature. Or they may refer to personal powers—to some of the "principalities and powers" (Eph. 6:12), to satanic forces that will be shaken up by divine action. "Then," without any long delay, "they will see the Son of man," that is, those living on earth will see the Messiah. His coming will be visible to all.

"Coming in clouds with great power and glory," probably refers not to natural clouds but to something like the "cloud of the Presence" that descended on the tabernacle in the wilderness and led the Israelites on their wilderness wanderings. Or, if one follows Wuest (p. 251), it is clouds of glorified saints and angels. Certainly in another description of this magnificent event in Revelation 19:11-16, Jesus is accompanied by innumerable hosts. And the Revelation passage more eloquently portrays the power and glory which are inherently His and which will envelop Him on that occasion. "Then," as He descends, He will send out His angels to gather to Himself the elect from the remotest parts of the earth. Presumably these are believers living on the earth at the time, tribulation saints who "endured to the end" of the Tribulation. These elect evidently are the "sheep" at the judgment which immediately takes place (according to Matt. 25:31ff.) and continue to live on earth during the kingdom (millennium that follows).

The need for watchfulness (13:28-37). The fig tree is not to be taken as symbolic of Israel here but as a literal tree that provides a lesson for anyone who will pay attention. As the branches of a fig tree begin to become tender and to leaf out, thereby heralding summer; just so, when anyone sees "these things" (especially events of the Tribulation) taking place, he will know that the return of Christ is near. "Coming events cast their shadows before them" (Burdick, p. 1017). "This generation" (v. 30) is frequently taken to refer literally to the generation to which Jesus was speaking and presumably then prophecies of the Olivet Discourse were fulfilled in some way in the destruction of Jerusalem. Such a view does not do justice to the details of Jesus' predictions, however. Others believe it refers to the preservation of the Jewish race, which would be preserved until all these things are fulfilled. Hiebert applies it to the generation living at the beginning of the events described in verses 14 and following, and holds that the verse teaches "the end-time crisis will not be of indefinite duration" (p. 331). Verse 31 asserts the absolute certainty of the whole prophetic scheme, and is thus a testimony to the inspiration of the Word and the sovereignty of God in controlling the movement of history.

But an outline of prophecy, signs of Christ's coming, and the certainty of prophetic fulfillment do not provide specifics as to when He will return. Date setting is always dangerous. In fact, He says "even the Son," does not know the time of the Second Coming. This is a surprising assertion but is evidently a result of His self-limitation. As Unger observes, "In Mark the Lord takes the place of complete humiliation as a Servant and the servant is, properly presented as he who 'knoweth not what his lord doeth' (Jn 15:15). After His servantship was discharged in death and He was raised in glory, the glorified Son omnisciently knew all, having this particular disclosure given Him (Rev. 1:1)" (*Handbook*, pp. 506-7). Since the time of Christ's coming is uncertain, it behooves His disciples to watch for His coming, to live in a state of expectancy. And what He is saying is not for the Twelve alone but is addressed "to all" His followers in every age (v. 37). While believers watch for the Master to return, each has "his particular task" to do (v. 34).

For Further Study

1. Note how Christ is the focus of attention in this chapter.

2. Note contrasts in this chapter, e.g., serenity and glory of the temple and prediction of its violent destruction, temporary nature of heavens and earth but permanence of God's Word.

3. What special value did the prediction of Christ's return in glory have for Jesus and the disciples at this time?

4. Show the various kinds of support that will be taken from the believer under persecution, forcing him to depend on God alone.

Chapter 16

The Self-sacrifice of the Servant
(Mark 14:1 – 15:47)

As Jesus finished His prophetic discourse on the Mount of Olives, He announced that in two days He would be delivered up for crucifixion (Matt. 26:2). About the same time members of the Sanhedrin—chief priests, scribes, elders of the people—gathered at Caiaphas' palace to plot how they could seize and kill Him (Matt. 26:3-4; Mark 14:1). The discussion did not concern whether but "how" to take Him; the decision already had been made that He must die (John 11:50-52). As the evening wore on, "they kept saying, 'It must not be at the feast, for there might be a riot'" (14:2, Williams). That is to say, they did not dare to move against Him openly during the Passover because they recognized His hold on the crowds and feared a riot in which they might actually be killed. Not only were many natives of Jerusalem impressed with Jesus' ministry and His claims, but also many of His followers from Galilee were in the city for Passover. Evidently while the Sanhedrin were still puzzling over how to get hold of Jesus, Judas came in and provided the solution to their problem. But before this Judas attended a dinner with the other members of the apostolic company in Bethany.

Anointing of Jesus (14:3-9). The event took place on Saturday night before the triumphal entry at the home of Simon the leper (John 12:1-11). Who he was we do not know; perhaps he was one of those whom Jesus had healed. At any rate, while the company was reclining in usual fashion around the table,[1] Mary, the sister of Martha and Lazarus, came in and anointed Him (John 12:3). She took an alabaster flask of pure nard (ointment from India), snapped the neck, and poured out all the con-

---

[1]Diners reclined on couches with their heads at the table, supported themselves on their left elbow, and ate with their right hand.

tents on His head and His feet and then wiped His feet with her hair. Judas evidently completely lost his patience over such a "wasteful" act (John 12:4-5) and brought on a general indignation among the disciples. Some idea of why this act created so much furor is gained from the observation that the ointment could have been sold for over 300 denarii. Since the denarius was the daily wage of a laborer, the value of this ointment was equal to almost a year's wages. The fact that Mary owned such a luxury is some indication of the economic status of the trio of friends where Jesus spent the last week of His life. Judas' observation of false concern was that the money might better have been given to the poor than thrown away in this fashion. The disciples "kept on scolding" Mary.

But Jesus defended Mary. "Let her alone," He ordered. "She has done a beautiful thing to me" (Beck), an act of pure devotion. He made it clear He was not insensitive to the poor, but said the poor would be among them always and they could help them "whenever you want to," "but you will not always have me." "She has done what she could. She has anointed my body beforehand for burial." What a startling pronouncement! If Mary caught the significance of Jesus' Passion announcements, she appears to have been the only one who did. In this connection, it is interesting to note that Mary did not go with the other women to the tomb to anoint Him on resurrection morning. Perhaps Mary had learned more about the Messiah sitting at His feet than anyone else had.

Here is this dear, devoted woman who realizes that the end is near. What could she do for Him? She could publicly demonstrate her devotion in the anointing. "She has done what she could." For her dedication Jesus would honor her by seeing to it that wherever the gospel is preached her devotion would be recognized. "Wherever the gospel is preached in the whole world" (NASB) is a fantastic statement, viewed in this context! Apprehension is beginning to grip the hearts of the entire company of Jesus' followers. Jesus has made it abundantly clear that He is to die in Jerusalem. When it looks like the end of everything, He intimates it is only the beginning—the gospel is to be preached in the whole world.

Contract for betrayal (14:10-11). Still smarting over Jesus' rebuke for his attitude toward Mary's anointing, Judas apparently went out that very night to confer with the chief priests—Caiaphas and Annas— "to betray him to them." Immediately the question arises as to why he would do such a thing. A simplistic approach is to say that "Satan entered into Judas" (Luke 22:3) and impelled him to do it.

But an explanation that attempts to incorporate a variety of factors might run something like this. Perhaps at the beginning Judas shared the hope of many other Israelites in a coming Messiah. But like them his thoughts centered on a political deliverer and his self-aggrandizing nature may have led him to join the band of disciples with the hope of a position of importance in the new kingdom. But gradually he grew at odds with Jesus and finally betrayed Him. Increasing antipathy may have come from a variety of sources. To begin with, if one accepts the likely view that "Iscariot" refers to his home, "of Kerioth," a village south of Hebron, then he was the only one of the disciples from Judea; all the rest were Galileans. This fact may have brought on certain frictions. Second, his business ability earned for him the position of treasurer of the group; and seemingly he grew ever more greedy. Along with the way he apparently embezzled funds entrusted to him (John 12:6). His greed was fully displayed in the anointing incident. Third, he gradually came to realize that the kingdom would not be political but spiritual; so his dreams for power were blasted. Now he concluded that the end was near and he decided to make the best of a bad situation by betraying Jesus for a price. Possibly the rebuke at Mary's anointing of Jesus was only the proverbial straw that broke the camel's back and precipitated action on Judas' part.

When he went to the chief priests, they rejoiced. The problem they had been struggling with for hours was on its way toward solution. He proposed a monetary reward for the betrayal and they agreed, giving him thirty pieces of silver (cf. Zech, 11:12), either as earnest money or full payment. If it was earnest money, he never received the rest because he came later to break the agreement and returned what he had received. The denomination of the coins is not given. If it was the denarius, the daily wage of a worker, the thirty working days would equal six five-day weeks for a modern worker. At a salary of $10,000 a year, the equivalent would be about $1,200. If another coin were chosen the total easily could run to four times that amount. At any rate, from that time on, "He began to look for a good opportunity to betray him to them." He had made the agreement and it was up to him to suggest a course of action to the chief priests.

Preparation for Passover (14:12-16). On the day "when they killed the passover [lamb]," i.e., Thursday, evidently in the morning, the disciples came to Jesus, no doubt while they were still in Bethany, for instructions on where to prepare the Passover. Perhaps by now they were getting anxious because time was growing short. The lamb was to be killed that afternoon and the Passover meal was to be eaten after sundown. Much preparation had to be made and they had received no instructions. In response, Jesus sent two of the disciples, Peter and John (Luke 22:8), into the city with specific instructions. First, they would see a man carrying a pitcher (jar) of water, a most unusual occurrence in a society where women always did this kind of work. No doubt he would be a servant, for they were to follow him to his destination and then speak to the owner of the house. They were to tell the owner: "The Teacher says: My appointed time is near. I am going to celebrate the Passover with my disciples at your house" (Matt. 26:18, NIV). Moreover, "The Teacher asks: Where is my guest room, where I may eat the Passover with my disciples?" (Mark 14:13, NIV). Certainly the owner of the house would know who the Teacher was and presumably would understand also that "my appointed time" referred to the Passion, which indicates intimate knowledge indeed. The owner of the house would respond by putting at the disciples' disposal a large upper room already furnished and prepared. That is, it would already have couches and other facilities adequate for the Passover. And an upper room would give the privacy Jesus wanted. There they were to prepare the Passover—see to the killing and roasting of the lamb and the provision of bread and other necessities. Peter, presumably Mark's informant, was impressed that everything turned out "just as He had told them."

Although it is possible that Jesus had made prior arrangements for the use of these facilities, the language of instruction to the disciples does not indicate that such was the case. Probably this was an illustration of Jesus' foreknowledge and preparation was made in the heart of the owner rather than through human arrangements. Evidently this secretive procedure was designed to prevent Judas and the Sanhedrin from disturbing Jesus' last hours with His disciples. In whose house they met neither Scripture nor tradition ventures to suggest. One might guess that it was Mark's house, on the supposition that the young man who fled the arrest scene in the garden (Mark 14:51-52) was John Mark. Possibly Mark followed Jesus and the other disciples when they left his house late at night and had time only to pull a linen cloth about him as he followed the company to the garden.

The Passover (14:17-21). Evidently when Peter and John had completed preparations for the Passover, they returned to Bethany to inform Jesus of the fact. After sunset He walked with the Twelve to the appointed place for the meal that was always eaten at night. Since the crowds of pilgrims that were in the city were busy with their own Passover celebrations, their travels passed unnoticed.

As they "were reclining" around the Passover table (students of Leonardo da Vinci take note), Jesus dropped a bombshell: "One of you will betray me—one who is eating with me" (v. 18, NIV). Immediately a pall of gloom and grief settled over the gathering and, as the Greek indicates, one by one in rapid succession they asked Jesus, "It is not I, is it?," fearing that in one of their weaker moments they might be capable of such a thing. Some commentators view verse 20 as a public statement, designed to indicate how despicable it was that someone who was on such intimate terms with Jesus could do such a thing. Others relate this to the scene in John 13:23ff. and consider it to be a private statement made to John. But Jesus is not at the mercy of a betrayer or a successful plot, "The Son of Man is going away, as the Scriptures say of Him" (v. 21, Williams), in fulfillment of Old Testament prophecy. However, "Nonexistence would have been preferable to the fearful fate awaiting the betrayer" (Hiebert, p. 350). At this point Judas left the company, as John makes clear (John 13:30).

Institution of the Lord's Supper (14:22-25). During the course of the Passover meal, "while they were eating," without waiting for the table to be cleared, "Jesus took bread," the unleavened flat cakes that would have been on the table, "gave thanks," uttered a blessing over the bread, "broke it" for distribution, and said to the disciples, "Take it; this is my body." Since He was still reclining with them very much alive, the most logical explanation of what He meant was, "this represents my body." It is foreign to the whole scene to suggest that the bread is the body of Christ in any literal sense.

Then He took the cup (one of the four cups at the Passover feast), uttered a blessing over it, and gave it to them; they all drank from the same cup. Then Jesus went on to explain, "This is my blood which ratifies the covenant, the blood which is to be poured out for many" (v. 24, Williams). The covenant was a new covenant (see Jer. 31:31-34); as the old covenant was ratified by blood so the new one would be ratified in the same way. The term for covenant does not express an agreement between equal parties but an arrangement sovereignly ordered by God; man may accept or reject at his peril. Blood to be poured out alludes to

His violent death, and "for many" (*on behalf of* or *instead of* many) clearly teaches the substitutionary nature of Christ's death, unto the remission of sins (Matt. 26:28). The one dies for the multitude to settle the sin problem once and for all. The end was near; He would no more drink with them in this present age, but would in the future when the kingdom would be established in all its glory.

   Prophecy of failure and denial (14:26-31). At the conclusion of the Passover-Lord's Supper, Jesus and the disciples sang a hymn, no doubt a portion of the Hallel Psalms (Pss. 115–118), and crossed the Kidron Valley to the Mount of Olives. On the way Jesus made a dire prediction of failure on the part of the disciples, especially of Peter's denial. On the basis of accounts in Luke 22:31-34 and John 13:36-38, Hiebert holds that Jesus first made this prediction in the upper room and then repeated it on the way to Gethsemane (p. 354). Jesus said that all "would be caused to stumble because of me," that their faith would be staggered by the events of the night and they would "fall away" (RSV, NIV). He supports this assertion by quotation of Zechariah 13:7, which refers to the striking down of the shepherd and the scattering of the sheep as "part of a refining process which will result in the creation of a new people of God" (Lane, 511) and the opening of a fountain for the cleansing of "the house of David and to the inhabitants of Jerusalem" (Zech. 13:1).

   Although the shepherd will be struck down and the sheep scattered in Judea, the Shepherd will be raised up again and the flock regathered in Galilee (Mark 14:28). But on this occasion as on so many others before, the disciples were so overwhelmed with predictions of Jesus' departure or death and its consequences that they failed to notice the promise of resurrection and restoration.

   As usual, explosive Peter stands strong in his self-assurance, in his own fancied strength. He dissociates himself from the failure and weakness of others; he will not stumble and fall. Jesus informs him that He knows better; this very night, "before the cock crows twice, you will disown me three times." The time is designated either in terms of a specific time period in the morning before dawn known to any rural person, or in connection with an incident that was to occur (see v. 72). Peter's vehement protestation of faithfulness to Jesus was matched by his equally vehement denial of the Master later in the night.

   Agony in the garden (14:32-42). As Jesus and the disciples went out of Jerusalem to the Mount of Olives (v. 26), "they came to a place called Gethsemane," meaning *oil press*. This olive orchard (called a garden in

John 18:1) was located somewhere on the western slope of the Mount of Olives, and the present Franciscan Garden and the Russian Orthodox Garden above it both may have been part of it. Probably surrounded by a stone wall, it was a favorite haunt of Jesus and His disciples while in Jerusalem. The fact that Jesus went there now shows that He was no longer trying to evade Judas (John 18:2). Entering the garden, Jesus commanded the disciples, "Sit here until I have prayed" (NASB), until I have finished praying. Then Jesus separated Peter, James, and John from the rest of the disciples and took them with Him a little deeper into the garden. Lane suggests that special attention to these three here was not evidence of privilege but was to point up their failure to understand what it meant to be identified with Jesus' sufferings and share His destiny. Peter had just protested his loyalty (14:29,31) and James and John had claimed ability to drink of Jesus' cup (10:38-40) (Lane, p. 515). But it could be argued just as cogently that in His hour of extremity He craved their sympathetic companionship.

He "began to be deeply agitated and distressed." As He was now brought face to face with the terrors of Calvary, which He had viewed at a distance for so long, Jesus entered into a whole new emotional state. He shared something of His apprehension with the three: His soul was so overwhelmed with sorrow that it threatened to crush out His life. He was beginning to enter into the agony of what it meant to bear the penalty of sin for the human race, to suffer the total alienation of God in judgment on that sin. So He asked the three to "watch," remain awake and alert, "with me" (Matt. 26:38), presumably to provide comfort and support in His aloneness.

Then He went forward about a stone's throw (Luke 22:41) and prostrated Himself on the ground (see Matt. 26:39). He "repeatedly prayed" that "if it were possible the hour might pass Him by" (NASB) or that "He might escape the hour of agony" (Williams). "The hour" was the time when in God's plan He was to die for the sins of the world. Lenski paraphrases the thought, "if it is possible to redeem the world without passing through this hour of suffering and death" (p. 636). "Abba" is Aramaic and "Father" its Greek equivalent. "This cup" has the same general reference point as "this hour"—the cup of agony, physical and spiritual, involved in bearing the guilt of a lost world. This is a cry to achieve salvation of the world by some other means if possible. But immediately He submits His will to that of the Father (John 5:30; 6:38; Heb. 5:7-8).

After His first prayer session, Jesus returned to the three to find them sleeping and addressed Peter as the leader of the group and as the one who had been most vocal in protesting his self-sufficiency in standing by Christ. However, He calls him by his natural name, "Simon," perhaps to draw attention to his humanness and weakness. But as is clear from verse 38, Jesus was more concerned for the disciples than He was for their failure in supporting Him. "Keep watching and praying, that you may not come into temptation" (NASB) urges to alertness and drawing upon divine resources, especially in preparation for the crisis hours to follow. "The spirit," their higher spiritual nature, is willing to express loyalty and service to the Master; but "the flesh," the old nature, is weak and unable to do so. The higher spiritual nature needs the help of God to be victorious over the downward pull of the old nature.

A second time Jesus went to prayer with the Father and used much the same words as before. Again Jesus returned to the disciples. It is absolutely remarkable that in His severe agony Jesus should have such great concern for His disciples. In fact, Mark's focus of attention is almost more on the sleeping disciples than on the suffering Messiah. This time He found them sleeping more soundly than before: "their eyes were weighted down" with sleep. The shamefaced disciples had no response, no excuse for their lethargy in the face of His sorrowful reproach.

Then Jesus went to prayer a third time (Matt. 26:44) and returned to find them still sleeping. What He says this time is hard to translate with certainty. Probably it is an ironical reproach, "Sleep on now and take your rest" (KJV). Lane prefers to translate "it is enough" as "it is settled" (p. 514). There is no need for further prayer to the Father. The Son of man will have to bear the sins of the world. His hour has arrived at last. "The Son of man is being betrayed into the hands of sinners"; the act is in process. These two statements should be enough to awaken them. All the dire predictions about His passion are about to be fulfilled. "Sinners" probably refers to the wicked members of the Sanhedrin. "Get up, let us be going. Look! here comes my betrayer" (Williams, v. 42).

Betrayal and arrest of Jesus (14:43-52). While Jesus was still urging the disciples to full alert, Judas came leading a crowd into the Garden. It is superfluous for Mark to identify him as "one of the Twelve," but the reference underscores the horror of his deed. Some had "clubs," temple police; and others had "swords," a band of Roman soldiers (John 18:12), which Lenski claims would have numbered about 200 (p. 645). Soldiers could be obtained by a request of the high priest in the event a dangerous person was to be apprehended. Because there were so many pilgrims in the city, a show of force would have been wise to prevent any of Jesus' friends from stirring up a riot and rescuing Him. Then there were representatives of the Sanhedrin in the crowd; all three elements of the Sanhedrin are mentioned: high priests, scribes, and elders.

Judas himself had devised a sign that would distinguish for the soldiers which one of the twelve men before them was Jesus of Nazareth. It is not clear whether Jesus' address to the crowd came before or after Judas's kiss.[2] At any rate, as Jesus identified Himself, many of the crowd were thrown to the ground by some divine force; and Jesus asked that His disciples be allowed to go free (John 18:2-10). As the parallel account in John indicates, Jesus voluntarily delivered Himself into the hands of His captors. But Peter had meant it when he said he would stand by Jesus. He drew a sword and took aim at Malchus, servant of the high priest (John 18:10), probably intending to split his head open. But the man no doubt ducked and only lost an ear; Jesus restored that (Luke 22:51).[3]

Then Jesus addressed the crowd further, evidently members of the Sanhedrin or the temple police this time, and protested the manner of His arrest (Mark 14:48-49). He, a harmless teacher, had taught often in the temple. They could have taken Him there and need not have apprehended Him here like a common robber. Of course the protest would do no good and He did not intend that it should change anything. He was merely registering a point and then recognized that God was carrying out His prophetic plan, and He voluntarily put Himself in the hands of His captors. At this juncture the eleven fled. Hiebert observes, "When His words and action made it clear that Jesus would offer no resistance to His arrest, their faith in Him as Messiah collapsed. To stay with Him now would only involve them in His unexpected fate" (p. 366).

But there was one who did not leave Jesus immediately. An unnamed young man (judging from the Greek, about twenty years of age) "started to follow him," whether in the garden or later in the street is not clear. Apparently awakened by the clamor of the crowd, he had simply come along in a loose sleeping garment or had thrown a sheet around

---

[2] It is popularly assumed that Judas's kiss involved an embrace, but the common way of showing respect to a rabbi was by kissing his hand (see Hiebert, p. 364).

[3] The disciples had two Roman short swords (Luke 22:38). How they got them and how many Jews were permitted to carry them is not known.

him. The fact that the cloth was of linen marks him as of the upper class. Who he was is not known but many have suspected that this was John Mark himself, the author of the Gospel. In the event that the passover meal was held at Mark's house, it is possible that Judas had led the band there looking for the Master and had then moved on to the garden. Mark may have been awakened by the racket and have rushed out to see what was going on. At any rate, some sought to apprehend this follower of Jesus. When they grabbed hold of his covering, he fled naked into the night and Jesus was left absolutely alone to face His accusers. The aloneness of the Master is the real point of the episode; it is not necessarily the author's way of leaving his autograph.

Jesus before the Sanhedrin (14:53-65). After Jesus was bound in the garden of Gethsemane He was led away to Annas, former high priest, for a preliminary hearing (John 18:12-14, 19-24). While that was going on a hurried call went out to summon the Sanhedrin. When they gathered, Jesus was led away to face the reigning high priest, Caiaphas, son-in-law of Annas, and the Sanhedrin. It is at this point that the Mark narrative picks up. Meanwhile Peter had also followed at a distance and had finally summoned up courage to go to the high priest's palace, where the meeting of the Sanhedrin was going on. John had preceded him there and had gotten inside because he was acquainted with the high priest. John was also influential in getting Peter admitted to Caiaphas' palace (John 18:15-18). When he entered the door, he made his first denial that he knew Jesus (John 18:17). Mark 14:54 now represents Peter as sitting in the courtyard, with the temple police, warming himself by the fire.

Meanwhile, inside, the Sanhedrin or council was proceeding to take evidence, apparently in a strictly legal manner but with the bias of seeking "testimony against Jesus to put him to death" (v. 55). Apparently they had been setting the stage for this hearing for some time because on this short notice they were able to bring in "many" witnesses. But their testimony was false and inconsistent and therefore was invalidated (v. 56). After some of the more trivial charges stood unproved, other witnesses came in to allege that He had claimed He would destroy the temple and in three days build another. These individuals were referring to one of Christ's remarks made during His early Judean ministry when He cleansed the temple the first time (John 2:19). This was a serious charge, normally a capital offense. In fact, when Jeremiah had merely predicted that a catastrophe would overtake the temple, he was brought before the royal court as a criminal worthy of death (Jer.

26:1-19). But these witnesses also failed to provide substantial evidence.

Finally, in frustration the high priest addressed Jesus Himself, hoping either to trip Him up in some inconsistency or to secure an admission or a pronouncement that would clinch the case. His first approach was to try to get Jesus to respond to some of the charges of witnesses. To these He had nothing to say, retaining a dignified silence before the spurious self-refuting testimony. Then the high priest decided to ask Him point blank, "Are you the Christ [the Messiah], the Son of the Blessed?" Matthew makes it clear that the high priest had placed Jesus under solemn oath to answer one way or the other. To answer no would be to lie and to bring ruin on His cause and on humanity forever; to answer yes was to saddle Him with self-incriminating evidence that would seal His doom. Unequivocally Jesus replied, "I am," admitting His messiahship. Then He made a most astounding claim: "You will see the Son of Man sitting at the right hand of the Mighty One and coming on the clouds of heaven" (NIV). In effect, He is saying, "You who seek to judge Me will see Me sitting at the right hand of God and coming in glorious splendor to judge all people at the end time." He completely turns the tables on them.

Ripping his clothes (certainly not his gorgeous official robes), the high priest affected an attitude of horror at what he declared to be blasphemy. He refused to accept the validity of Christ's claims and considered Him to be a mere man. Lane observes, "A Messiah imprisoned, abandoned by his followers, and delivered helpless into the hands of his foes represented an impossible conception. Anyone who, in such circumstances, proclaimed himself to be the Messiah could not fail to be a blasphemer who dared to make a mockery of the promises given by God to his people" (p. 536).

Then Caiaphas put the question of Jesus' guilt to the whole council, and they unanimously "condemned him to be worthy of death." Having made their decision, the Sanhedrin engaged in conduct wholly unbecoming to men of their stature. To test His omniscience, they blindfolded Him and called on Him to tell who had hit Him. Rather than discrediting Him, "They only succeeded in demonstrating the awful depravity of the human heart" (Hiebert, p. 374).

Peter's denial of Jesus (14:66-72). In verse 66 the narrative returns to where it left off in verse 54. Apparently the interrogation of Peter was going on in the courtyard while the trial of Jesus was going on inside. As Peter warmed himself in the courtyard, the fire lit up his face enough for him to be recognized. Evidently the portress who had let him in recognized him first: "You also were with the Nazarene, this Jesus." "Also" probably refers to John who had arranged for her to let Peter in. Somewhere she had seen him with Jesus, but he denied the fact in the language of formal, legal denial used in rabbinical law. Uncomfortable where it was light enough for his face to be seen, Peter moved into the covered archway opening onto the street. "Then a cock crowed" is omitted in some manuscripts but perhaps belongs in the text here.

The maid later saw Peter in the entrance area and called attention of bystanders to the fact that he was one of the disciples. "But he repeatedly denied it" to the several standing around him. Then about an hour later, as Peter sought to lose himself in the crowd in the courtyard, several again accused him of being one of Jesus' disciples, of being a Galilean. This time "he began to curse and swear, 'I do not know this fellow [derogatory reference] you are talking about!'" (NASB). This does not mean that Peter used foul language, but rather, he called down curses on himself if he was not telling the truth and swore or took an oath that he was telling the truth. Then the cock crowed a second time. Apparently at that very moment the Sanhedrin had finished abusing Jesus and were turning Him over to the soldiers in the courtyard to abuse Him further. "The Lord turned and looked straight at Peter" (Luke 22:61, NIV). That look[4] broke him and reduced him to convulsive sobs. Henceforth Peter dropped completely out of sight until after the crucifixion.

Jesus before Pilate (15:1-15). Mark now turns from the religious to the political phase of Jesus' trial. "Very early in the morning" (v. 1, NIV), between five and six in the morning, the "whole" council or Sanhedrin met. Evidently with the chief priests taking the lead, all elements of the Sanhedrin, including scribes and elders, were present. There is no need to conclude, however, that every one of the seventy-one members attended. At least Joseph of Arimathæa and Nicodemus appear to have been absent. The Sanhedrin "passed a resolution" confirming the verdict of death which had been voted at the illegal night session. Apparently this was designed to fulfill the requirement of Jewish law that in capital cases a second session dealing with a case had to be held a day later in order to secure the death verdict. No doubt this meeting convened early in the morning, in order to get the case on the docket of

---

[4]Elizabeth Barrett Browning's *The Look* and *The Meaning of the Look* seek to interpret that moment when Jesus "looked at" Peter.

the Roman court, which met soon after daybreak.

Though Jesus had been bound in the garden, He must have been unfettered in Caiaphas's palace; now He is bound again for transfer to Pilate. The reason why He was sent to Pilate was that though the Sanhedrin could pass a death sentence, they could not execute a criminal; only Roman authorities could do that. Pilate, prefect[5] of Judea, ruled the province A.D. 26-36. As the chief Roman executive in the area, he could simply ratify the decision of the Sanhedrin or reverse it. If he had any thoughts about reversing it, he had to conduct what amounted to a new trial. After the Sanhedrin sent Jesus to Pilate, Judas was seized with remorse, returned the "blood money," and went out and hanged himself (Matt. 27:3-10).

The trial before Pilate was held either in Herod's palace or the fortress of the Antonia, probably the former. No charge of blasphemy against God would bring condemnation here; so the Sanhedrin revised the accusation in political terms. He was now accused of being guilty of fomenting revolution, forbidding payment of taxes to Caesar, and especially of claiming to be king of the Jews and thus guilty of treason against the Roman government (see Luke 23). The last is the only charge that got serious attention from Pilate and is the one on which Mark concentrates in verse 2. In response to Pilate's question of whether Jesus is really king of the Jews, He answers, "Yes, it is as you say" (v. 2, NIV). The statement is a rather guarded one, judging from the Greek text, and John 18:34-38 makes it clear that Jesus qualified His answer with an explanation of the nature of His kingdom. John also shows that Pilate's interrogation of Jesus was a private hearing after which the two went outside again to meet Jesus' accusers. When Pilate answered that he found Jesus innocent of their charges, the Sanhedrin hurled a barrage of accusations against Him; but Jesus remained absolutely silent (Isa. 53:7). Pilate was tremendously impressed with the quiet dignity of Jesus and His refusal to deal with their false charges.

Among the charges leveled against Jesus was one of stirring up trouble even in Galilee (Luke 23:5). That gave Pilate his out, he thought. Here was a chance to be relieved of this troublesome case which he preferred not to handle. Herod Antipas, ruler of Galilee, was in town; let him deal with the matter, since Jesus was really a Galilean anyway. But after a brief hearing Herod returned Jesus to Pilate's jurisdiction. Soon

---

[5]Properly the chief Roman official in Judea was called a prefect at this time. Later in the first century he was called a procurator.

Pilate had another course of action open to him. It was customary, and evidently had been long before Roman occupation of Palestine, to release from prison at Passover time someone whom the people chose. Apparently at this point some of the common people who had been watching this public outdoor trial sought to make good on this opportunity for clemency while Pilate was accessible to them; so they sent a delegation to ask him to honor the custom. Pilate thought it was his chance to get out of a box.

He would give them a choice of releasing one who was guilty of insurrection, and murder and robbery in the process, or Jesus (Matt. 27:17). Certainly, he thought, they would choose to release Jesus instead of the disreputable Barabbas. The way the question is put in Mark 15:9 clearly indicates that Pilate wanted to let Jesus go free. Pilate was trying to pit the common people against the Sanhedrin here; he understood that the Sanhedrin had launched a vendetta against Jesus because of "envy"—He was too influential with the masses (Mark 15:10). Apparently at this point Pilate received the urgent message from his wife recorded in Matthew 27:19. And his temporary absence gave opportunity to representatives from the Sanhedrin, predominantly the chief priests, to put pressure on the crowd to vote for Barabbas. How they persuaded them to make such a choice is not indicated. The degree of pressure or "lobbying" or excited agitation may be indicated by the words "stirred up" or "incited" or "shook up" the multitude. The decision left Pilate stunned and helpless; he somehow had the belief that the crowd would exonerate an evidently guiltless man.

Now Pilate still has Jesus on his hands. Instead of exercising the good sense or fortitude of handling the case himself, in his moment of uncertainty he put himself in the hands of the crowd and thus unwittingly in the hands of the Sanhedrin. When Pilate asked the crowd what he was to do with Jesus, presumably the Sanhedrin first, followed by the rest, yelled "Crucify him." The question has been asked as to how they reached such a decision on form of execution when stoning was a normal form of Jewish death sentence, beheading the Roman death for a citizen, and crucifixion for a slave or foreigner. Lenski finds the explanation in the fact "that the Jews had turned Jesus completely over to Pilate to be executed by him. The Romans had deprived them of the right of inflicting the death penalty, so they held Pilate to its infliction, and that would be by crucifixion alone" (p. 691). When Pilate sought to reason with the crowd (v. 14), they set up a fiercer clamor for Jesus' crucifixion.

Now Pilate has a mob action on his hands. Wishing to "satisfy" or "appease" indicates that he is now in the process of complete capitulation to them.

But as John indicates (19:1-15) Pilate tried one last effort to save Jesus—to try to move the crowd to pity by the terrible spectacle of flogging, which would have left His whole back side a bloody pulp. But that was not enough; they demanded His execution. So Pilate "handed him over to be crucified" (v. 15, NIV). When Pilate tried to wash his hands of responsibility in the matter, the people assumed the responsibility (Matt. 27:24-25). This is "not the trial before Pilate, but the trial of Pilate, for he stands self-revealed as he attempts in vain, first to avoid the issue, and then to escape responsibility for the decision" (Cole, p. 232). Pilate "was perfectly conscious of the wrongfulness of what he did, and thus but increases his guilt" (Cole, p. 236).

The Crucifixion (15:16-32). The die was cast. The process of crucifixion was now begun. As a prelude, "the soldiers," part of a non-Jewish guard Pilate brought with him from Caesarea, led Jesus away "into the courtyard of the governor's official residence." The flogging evidently took place outside the grounds; now Jesus is led into what amounts to the courtyard of the barracks. "And they call together the whole company of soldiers," understood to mean either a maniple of 200 or a cohort of 600. And they proceed to make sport of Jesus, to conduct an "uproarious masquerade" or "grotesque vaudeville" (Lane, p. 559). So this fellow claims to be a king! They will outfit Him like one. First comes the robe, apparently of scarlet (Matt. 27:28). The Greek word used in Mark represents a variety of colors, including purple, as rendered in some versions. Presumably the robe was an old cast-off scarlet cloak that once had belonged to a Roman soldier. The "crown of thorns" probably was intended to resemble the laurel wreath worn by the emperor or the gilded wreath of leaves worn by Hellenistic vassal kings. The soldiers twisted together some thorns to make a substitute for an official crown, which at the same time would look ridiculous and bring suffering to the wearer. The kind of thorn used is unknown; evidently it belonged to a bush or tree growing in the courtyard of the barracks. And they saluted Him, "Hail, king of the Jews," in imitation of the imperial salute, "Hail, Caesar." The verbs in verse 19 are all in the imperfect tense, showing continued action: they repeatedly hit Him on the head with a rod to drive the thorns in deeper, repeatedly spit at Him in derision, and repeatedly bowed the knee to Him in mock obeisance.

Finally they took off the mock regalia, put Jesus' own clothes back on Him, and an execution squad of four soldiers led Him out to be crucified (John 19:23). Lenski argues that Pilate had gone into the courtyard with the soldiers and ordered the mocking, and then brought Him out again to appear before the crowd. Hopefully by making the charges against Jesus to appear ridiculous, he could still protect Jesus against crucifixion; but it didn't work (Lenski, p. 695).

As the soldiers led Jesus outside the city to the place of crucifixion, His physical strength finally gave out; the frightful abuse had taken its toll. Since He was no longer able to carry His cross, they "impressed" a certain "Simon of Cyrene" and forced him to carry it. Simon was a Jew from the territory of Cyrene, now a part of Libya, who apparently had moved to Jerusalem and attended a synagogue along with other Jews from Cyrene (Acts 2:10; 6:9). He is identified as the father of Alexander and Rufus, evidently leaders in a church known to Mark's readers. Many identify Rufus with the man of the same name in Romans 16:13 and conclude that this experience of Simon helped lead him to salvation.

"They brought him upon the Golgotha place, which means place of a skull." The English word *Calvary* comes from the Latin *calvaria*, "a skull." "Upon the Golgotha place" seems to require a slight knoll and Golgotha (Aramaic for skull) seems to refer to the fact that its smooth, rounded top resembled a bald head or skull. Evidently it was a well-known place on the north or northwest of the city just outside the city wall. There are two suggestions for the location of Golgotha: the Church of the Holy Sepulcher and "Gordon's Calvary." Though the Church of the Holy Sepulcher now stands within the wall of Jerusalem, in recent years bits of evidence have come to light to demonstrate that Golgotha was outside the walls in Jesus' day; and a variety of indications give it an excellent claim to being the very spot of Golgotha. "Gordon's Calvary" was popularized as the site of the crucifixion late in the nineteenth century, but there is not much to support the identification.

Before the act of crucifixion the soldiers offered Jesus wine mixed with myrrh, which had an anaesthetic effect. But He refused it, wishing to have all His faculties unclouded as He assumed His task of bearing the sin of the whole world. Then they crucified Jesus, but no details of the process or of the terrible agonies involved are given. All that can be gleaned from the Gospels is that both His hands and feet were nailed to the cross (John 20:25; Luke 24:39, 40). The fact that an inscription appeared above His head leads to the conclusion that the form of the cross was the common Latin cross. Thus, His arms would have been stretched out along the crossbeam and His body would have rested on a little projection a foot or two above the earth. He would not therefore have been elevated above the milling crowd, contrary to the representations of most artists. The clothes of the crucified One fell to the soldiers, who parted His outer cloak into four parts along the seams and cast lots for the inner seamless garment of linen (John 19:23,24) and thus fulfilled the prophecy in Psalm 22:18: "They part my garments among them, and cast lots upon my vesture" (kjv).

Mark gives the time of crucifixion as "the third hour," the Jewish reckoning for 9:00 A.M. But John indicates that Pilate pronounced his verdict against Jesus "about the sixth hour" (19:14) or noon. No completely satisfactory solution to this problem has been offered, but Hiebert concludes: "The most probable solution is the view that John, writing in Asia Minor, used the Roman official mode of computation, reckoning from midnight, so that the sixth hour would be 6 A.M." (p. 392).

Commonly a placard ("superscription") bearing the name of the criminal and his crime was placed above the head of a condemned man and attached to the upright pole of the cross. On the way to the cross this placard was either carried before him or suspended from his neck. In this case, the name appeared as "Jesus of Nazareth" (John 19:19) and the crime was listed as "King of the Jews." Slight variations in the wording in the Gospels may result from the fact that it appeared in three languages. Pilate did not say, "He claimed to be king of the Jews" but he said that He was the king of the Jews. The chief priests protested to Pilate the nature of the wording (John 19:21-22) but he refused to change it. Thus he had his "last revenge on the Jews who had forced him into such a difficult position" (Cole, p. 239).

Jesus was crucified between two "robbers," guilty of more than thievery because theft was not a capital offense. Undoubtedly the crime was at least robbery combined with violence. And in this case reference seemingly is to men guilty of insurrection (see Mark 14:48 and John 18:40, where the same Greek word is used). Josephus, the first-century Jewish historian, applied the term to the Jewish sect of the Zealots, who had committed themselves to armed conflict against Rome and who standardly suffered crucifixion when caught by the Romans (Lane, p. 568). Likely these two men were involved in the same conspiracy as Barabbas (Mark 15:7). If so, the substitutionary death of Jesus is markedly evident, the one innocent of the charge of insurrection dies in the place of one guilty of it. This fact, coupled with some realization of who Jesus really was led to the conversion of one of the terrorists (Luke 23:41-43), even though initially both of them apparently hurled insults at Him (Mark 15:32). Jesus' crucifixion between these criminals was a fulfillment of prophecy (Isa. 53:12). Verse 28 is not in the best manuscripts of Mark and probably does not belong to the original.

"Those passing by" could refer simply to Jews from the city who were passing by this public execution place. But the nature of their taunts may indicate that they were a little better informed than the mob in general. Allusion to destruction of the temple and rebuilding it in three days was a charge levied earlier by members of the Sanhedrin or their attendants (14:58). "Repeatedly blasphemed him" is the literal translation, and shows they were not merely defaming a criminal but were actually blaspheming the Son of God. They shook their heads in derision (Ps. 22:7); certainly if He could rebuild the temple in three days, He could save Himself.

Whether or not verse 29 refers to members of the Sanhedrin, verse 31 certainly does. The chief priests and scribes (and elders, Matt. 27:41), not in direct address but mocking among themselves in Jesus' hearing, now congratulate themselves on their success in destroying the Nazarene. "He saved others; himself he cannot save." He performed miraculous acts on others and healed them, but Himself He cannot deliver. The implication is that if He really had the power of God upon Him he could now deliver Himself (see Matt. 27:43). But in this statement lies the essence of the gospel. If Jesus Christ is to save others from their sins, He cannot save Himself from death; only His substitutionary sacrifice could provide salvation for them. Next, the Sanhedrin jeer at Jesus' messianic claims and call on Him to demonstrate the truth of those claims by descending from the cross in a miraculous display of power. As is clear from other indications, the Sanhedrin would not have believed if Jesus had come down from the cross. They already had many signs in the many miracles He had performed; and He declared in the parable of the rich man and Lazarus (Luke 16:31) that they would not believe even if one came back from the dead to preach to them. When Jesus Himself did rise from the dead, they refused to believe it and did all they could to suppress news of the fact.

The death of Jesus (15:33-41). On various occasions in the past the Pharisees had asked for a special sign from heaven. Now they have their wish. At the "sixth hour," noon, when the sun was at its zenith, darkness suddenly came upon "the whole land," either the land of Israel or the whole earth (the Greek can mean either), and lasted until the "ninth hour," 3:00 P.M. There is no need to speculate here on the nature of the phenomenon or how it could have occurred. Clearly it was a super- natural cosmic sign involving God's judgment on sin. During all that time a blanket of silence covered Jesus' sufferings. Finally He cried out, "Eloi, Eloi, lama sabachthani?" which is Aramaic and which Mark renders in Greek for his Greco-Roman readers: "My God, my God, for what purpose did you forsake me?" This is a quotation from Psalm 22:1, one of the greatest of the Messianic Psalms. This quote gives a clue as to what was going on during those awful hours of darkness. As translated, the proper rendering here is "did you forsake." The forsaking was an event now past; evidently the Father's forsaking of Jesus was going on during those three hours and He was being made sin for us (2 Cor. 5:21; Gal. 3:13). Because He was suffering as a human being the penalty human beings deserved, He cried not "my Father" but "my God." And He did not ask why the penalty or judgment had to fall, but rather "what purpose" was served in its coming in this way.

The loud cry of Jesus could be heard for a distance. Some, evidently Jews, who were standing nearby said, "He is calling for Elijah." This observation is better understood by referring to Matthew 27:46, where the Hebrew rendering of the question appears: "Eli, Eli." Presumably Jesus spoke in Hebrew on this occasion and the response was a misun- derstanding of a deliberate effort at ridicule. "This one is calling for Elijah to come and help him!" Evidently at this point Jesus said, "I thirst" (John 19:28), and a soldier dipped a sponge in a jar of wine vinegar and held it on a stick for Jesus to drink. Soldiers and workers found wine vinegar more refreshing than water and this jar no doubt was kept for the soldiers' own use. Jesus sucked on the sponge briefly (John 19:30); this time the wine offered was not mixed with a drug. Some standing there again spoke derisively, "Let's see if Elijah comes to save him" (NIV, Matt. 27:49). Then "Jesus uttered a loud cry" (NASB), evidently the triumphant cry of John 19:30: "It is finished," committed His spirit to the Father (Luke 23:46), and died.

Now Mark comments on some events and people connected with the death of Jesus. First, the veil or curtain between the holy place and holy of holies in the temple was torn in two from top to bottom. This was a very thick curtain and the destruction evidently was supernatural. The significance of this startling development appears in Hebrews 6:19-20; 10:19-22. Second, Mark records the reaction of the centurion (commander of a contingent of 100 men) in charge of the crucifixion. He had "stood facing him" and no doubt observed His every move during the long ordeal. The Roman concluded: "Truly this was God's son." The centurion had heard the charge that Jesus claimed to be the Son of God, and he had heard Jesus address God as Father, and had come to believe it was true. But He "was" God's son: the centurion thought He now was no more. Third, Mark comments on some women watching from a distance—witnesses of a different sort. There was Mary of Magdala on the western shore of the Sea of Galilee, Mary the mother of James the less and Joses, and Salome—evidently the wife of Zebedee and mother of James and John (Matt. 27:56). These women "kept ministering" to Him in Galilee (cf. Luke 8:1-3), no doubt providing sums for the common treasury which Judas had supervised. These women became significant witnesses to the death (vv. 40-41), burial (v. 47) and resurrection of Jesus (16:1).

Burial of Jesus (15:42-47). "Evening having already come," the first evening from mid-afternoon to sunset, "because it was the Preparation," the day to get ready for Sabbath and no work could be done after sunset, Joseph of Arimathaea rushed to get permission to bury Jesus. Among the Jews even convicted criminals were not to remain unburied after sunset. Joseph from Arimathaea, was now living in Jerusalem and had prepared a tomb for himself (Matt. 27:60). A member of the Sanhedrin (Luke 23:51), a man of wealth (Matt. 27:57), and a secret disciple of Jesus (John 19:38), Joseph went "boldly" to Pilate. In the light of all that had happened, this took great courage indeed. Pilate marveled at Jesus' early death and summoned the centurion to confirm the fact. Assured that it was indeed true, he granted the body to Joseph. It was no doubt after 4:00 P.M. by that time, and Joseph had to work fast. As a man of wealth, he had servants to help accomplish the necessary tasks—to buy linen cloth, take the body down from the cross, wash it for burial, wind it in the cloth, lay it on a shelf in his own rock-cut tomb, and then to roll a stone against the door. Nicodemus also helped in the preparations, especially by providing the spices to anoint the body (John 19:38-42). Mary Magdalene and Mary the mother of Joses were witnesses to the location of the tomb and were important testimony to the fact that the right tomb was empty after resurrection morning.

For Further Study

1. Trace the attitudes toward Jesus in Mark 14-15.

2. Note the various steps leading to the crucifixion.

3. Make an observation on the prominence of Peter; note the steps in his downfall.

4. Cite indications which show that Jesus was Deity (note claims and indirect references).

5. Show how predictions in the passion references are fulfilled in the events that take place here.

Chapter 17

The Resurrection of the Servant
(Mark 16:1-20)

A dead Christ could contribute nothing to the real solution of mankind's spiritual problem. Martyrs to religious causes had come along before and would do so in the future. Ethical systems had been concocted before and would be again. What was needed was a solution to the sin problem which men and women could not provide in their own strength. What was needed was an ever-living divine shepherd who could care for and lead His people. What was needed was a religion that would provide for life beyond the grave—a future glorious life in the presence of God.

The resurrection of Christ provides the assurance that the penalty for sin has been paid and need not be paid again. Resurrection from the dead furnishes a new resurrection power that enables believers to live a whole new kind of life and makes old merit-building ethical systems obsolete. The resurrection of Jesus provides an ever-living intercessor (Heb. 7:25) with God and an ever-living shepherd to guide, guard, and feed His people. His resurrection establishes the basis for ours (1 Cor. 15) and is the guarantee that we shall ever live with Him, will ever enjoy Him, and will ever rule with Him.

Women at the tomb (16:1-8) But unfortunately neither the disciples nor Jesus' larger group of followers expected Him to rise from the dead, and they had a little difficulty believing it after it happened. Even before sundown on Friday some of the women had started preparing aromatic oils and other ointments to anoint Jesus' body. Then they broke off their activity on the Sabbath as good law-abiding Jews (Luke 23:55-56). When the Sabbath was over they went out to buy more spices with which to anoint Jesus. They were not planning to embalm Him as some translators and commentators suggest, for Jews did not do that. They would pour oils over the head of the deceased in an act of loving adoration and would leave perfumes to offset the odor of decomposition.

Early in the morning on Sunday, while it was still dark, the women started out for the tomb. Apparently they arrived just after sunrise. Those in the group were Mary Magdalene, Mary the mother of James, Salome, Joanna (Luke 24:10), and others. There were no men along. As they neared the tomb, they suddenly remembered the stone that had been rolled to the door and began to wonder who would roll it away for them. They really would have been upset if they had known about the sealing of the door and the posting of the guard (Matt. 27:62-66). When their downcast eyes looked up, they saw the stone "rolled back," not to one side in the usual easier way, but back away from the entrance. The size of the stone indicates the wealth of Joseph and the large size of the opening. Apparently one could almost stand up while entering.

Even though the tomb stood open, the women still had no inkling of the Resurrection. On entering the anteroom of this large family-type tomb, they started looking for the body. Finding none, "they were awestruck" when two angels, previously invisible, now revealed themselves (Luke 24:3-4). Mark speaks of only one young man, probably the spokesman, clothed in a dazzlingly white robe bespeaking a kind of glory. The angel did not ask the women what they wanted but informed them that Jesus of Nazareth, the crucified one, was risen from the dead. For proof he pointed out the stone slab on which Jesus had been laid. All that remained were the empty bands of linen that had been wound around His body (John 20:6). "Go, tell." "Their faithfulness had qualified them to be the first recipients of the good news . . ." (Hiebert, p. 410). And the fact that the women told the disciples about the Resurrection helps to underscore the falsehood of the report that the disciples had stolen the body and hid it somewhere (Matt. 28:13). "And Peter." What a marvelous message of grace! After the terrible hours of anguish during Friday and Saturday, weeping his heart out over his betrayal, Peter hears the word that he is still considered to be a member of the band of disciples. Forgiveness and restoration are available to him. This touch would be expected in a Gospel written under the influence of Peter.

The disciples can expect to meet Jesus in Galilee "as he said." In Mark 14:28 Jesus had clearly foretold His resurrection and the fact that He would precede and meet His disciples in Galilee. Evidently that fact had not registered with them because they apparently did not expect the Resurrection. Now He reminded them of it. But just in case that announcement required too much faith, He would appear to them a couple of times in Jerusalem (that night and the following Sunday) before the preannounced meeting in the North. Having been in the presence of divine power and glory, the women were awestruck and terrified. They ran from the tomb and "said nothing to anyone." This could be interpreted as meaning they were too overwhelmed and confused to say anything to anyone, including the disciples, or that they were too dazed and overwhelmed to speak to anyone until they had delivered the message to the disciples and had had a chance to collect their wits. Perhaps both are true. It may have taken them a little while to pull themselves together before they even went to the disciples, and probably they did not speak to anyone else about these matters until they had seen the disciples.

The ending of Mark. The question of the ending of Mark is one of the most thorny in all of New Testament scholarship. The best manuscripts stop at verse 8. The great scholar Eusebius of Caesarea, writing in the fourth century, said that nearly all copies of the Gospel ended with verse 8. Jerome, translator of the Vulgate, said almost the same thing shortly after A.D. 400. Moreover, many argue that verses 9-20 are not in the same style as the rest of the book. So the tendency of modern textual scholars is to omit these verses.

But to end Mark at verse 8 makes it look unfinished or at least very abrupt in its ending. Many are not troubled by that because Mark's style is rather abrupt. A few early versions include a short summary ending that has very weak manuscript support and no real claim to authenticity. It reads as follows: "But they reported briefly to Peter and those with him all that they had been told. And after this, Jesus himself sent out by means of them, from east to west, the sacred and imperishable proclamation of eternal salvation" (RSV).

One should not be too hasty in throwing out Mark 16:9-20, however. Justin Martyr, Irenaeus, and Tatian witnessed to its inclusion in the second century. And the earliest translations—the Latin, Syriac, and Coptic—all include it. In his new study on the subject, Farmer pleads for keeping the question open and thinks that present-known evidence probably will not permit a final conclusion on the matter (pp. ix, 109). Hopefully new manuscripts bearing on the question will yet come to light.

The long ending of Mark (16:9-20). This section provides a summary of some resurrection appearances (vv. 9-14), records Christ's commission to His followers (vv. 15-18) and reports His ascension (vv. 19-20). In the discussion of the resurrection appearances emphasis seems to be on unbelief. The disciples refused to believe the story of Mary Magdalene (v. 11) and the two on the road to Emmaus (v. 13), and had some problems with Jesus Himself which called forth a stern rebuke (v. 14). It is useful to think about these references when dealing with those who claim that the idea of the Resurrection was concocted by Mary Magdalene and some other excitable women and embraced by gullible disciples eager to pawn off an old wives' tale. The disciples themselves at first seemed to have regarded the appearances of Christ as phantom appearances (cf. Luke 24:37) and had a difficult time persuading themselves Jesus really had risen from the dead. The appearance to Mary Magdalene is described more at length in John 20:11-18. Here the point is made that she was the first one to whom Jesus appeared and that from her seven demons had been cast. The account of Jesus' self-revelation to the two men on the road to Emmaus occurs in more detail in Luke 24:13-35. When Jesus met with the disciples He "reproached" them for their unbelief because they refused to accept the testimony of eyewitnesses concerning the Resurrection.

The commission of verses 15-18 is longer and more debated than that of Matthew 28:19-20. In spreading the gospel, no part of the world is to be omitted. One is to proclaim as a herald the good news about Jesus Christ to all mankind. "He who believes [inward reception] and has been baptized" as a testimony of his belief "shall be saved"—a passive pointing to salvation as a work of God alone. Then certain signs accompany those who believe, signs which will accredit the message and will be found in the church but will not necessarily be equally enjoyed by all in the church. As is clear from the classic passage on gifts in 1 Corinthians 12-14, gifts or powers are sovereignly bestowed by God Himself and He does not bestow the same gifts on all. Casting out demons, speaking in tongues, and healing appear in other passages. Taking up serpents and drinking a poison are more questionable matters. Apparently both acts involve promise of divine protection in the line of duty. It is hard to stretch either one to deliberate snake handling or drinking of poison. If one is tempted to claim special powers in these two areas, he should remember that this is, after all, disputed Scripture and one should not base doctrine or practice on it.

"After the Lord Jesus had spoken to them" (NIV). When His post-resurrection ministry was completed, He ascended into heaven. This much of verse 19 the disciples visually observed. The last half of the verse, "sat down at the right hand of God," is attested by Peter (Acts 2:33-35) and Stephen (Acts 7:56). The last verse is a summary statement of what happened after the Ascension: it speaks at the same time of the faithfulness of the disciples in their ministry and the faithfulness of God in empowering them to succeed in the proclamation of the Word of God. "They went out and preached everywhere, and the Lord worked with them and confirmed the Word by the wonderful proofs that went with it" (v. 20, Beck).

For Further Study

1. Make a careful analysis of Mark 16:9-20 to discover if any detail of doctrine or historical fact would be lost from the Christian message if this passage were omitted from the New Testament.

2. With the aid of a Bible dictionary or encyclopedia or book on Bible doctrine, note the various theories of the Resurrection that have been suggested by those who prefer not to accept a literal resurrection of Jesus Christ. Can you find answers to these theories?

3. With the aid of a Bible dictionary or encyclopedia try to construct in chronological order a list of the resurrection appearances of Jesus recorded in the New Testament.

4. List ways in which you believe you are helping to fulfill the Great Commission.

Bibliography

Alford, Henry, *The Greek Testament*. With revisions by Everett F. Harrison (Chicago: Moody Press, 1958).

Barclay, William, *The Gospel of Mark* (Philadelphia: The Westminster Press, 1954).

Bruce, Alexander B., "The Synoptic Gospels," in *The Expositor's Greek Testament*. Reprint Edition (Grand Rapids: Wm. B. Eerdmans Publishing Company, n. d.).

Burdick, Donald W., "The Gospel According to Mark," in *The Wycliffe Bible Commentary* (Chicago: Moody Press, 1962).

Chadwick, G. A., "The Gospel According to St. Mark," in *The Expositor's Bible*. Reprint Edition (Grand Rapids: Wm. B. Eerdmans Publishing Company, 1943).

Cole, Alan, *The Gospel According to St. Mark* (Grand Rapids: Wm. B. Eerdmans Publishing Company, 1961).

Earle, Ralph, *The Gospel According to Mark* (Grand Rapids: Zondervan Publishing House, 1957).

Farmer, William R., *The Last Twelve Verses of Mark* (Cambridge: Cambridge University Press, 1965).

Guthrie, Donald, *New Testament Introduction* (Chicago: InterVarsity Press, 1965).

Harrison, Everett F., *Introduction to the New Testament* (Grand Rapids: Wm. B. Eerdmans Publishing Company, rev. ed., 1971).

Hiebert, D. Edmond, *An Introduction to the New Testament* (Chicago: Moody Press, Vol. 1, 1975).

_____, *Mark: A Portrait of the Servant* (Chicago: Moody Press, 1974).

Jamieson, Robert; Fausset, Andrew R.; and Brown, David, *A Commentary, Critical, Experimental, and Practical on the Old and New Testaments*. Reprint Edition (Grand Rapids: Wm. B. Eerdmans Publishing Company, 1945).

Jensen, Irving L., *Mark: A Self-Study Guide* (Chicago: Moody Press, 1972).

Lane, William L., *The Gospel According to Mark* (Grand Rapids: Wm. B. Eerdmans Publishing Company, 1974).

Lenski, R. C. H., *The Interpretation of St. Mark's Gospel* (Minneapolis: Augsburg Publishing House, 1946).

Maclear, G. F., *The Gospel According to St. Mark* (Cambridge: Cambridge University Press, 1904).

Plummer, Alfred, *The Gospel According to St. Mark* (Cambridge: Cambridge University Press, 1938).

Ryle, J. C., *Expository Thoughts on the Gospels*. Reprint Edition (Grand Rapids: Zondervan Publishing House, 1956).

Ryrie, Charles C., *You Mean the Bible Teaches That* (Chicago: Moody Press, 1974).

St. John, Harold, *An Analysis of the Gospel of Mark* (London: Pickering & Inglis, 1956).

Scroggie, W. Graham, *A Guide to the Gospels* (London: Pickering & Inglis, 1948).

Stonehouse, Ned B., *The Witness of Matthew and Mark to Christ* (Philadelphia: The Presbyterian Guardian, 1944).

Thompson, Ernest T., *The Gospel According to Mark* (Richmond: John Knox Press, 1954).

Unger, Merrill F., *Unger's Bible Handbook* (Chicago: Moody Press, 1966).

Vincent, Marvin R., *Word Studies in the New Testament:* Reprint Edition (Grand Rapids: Wm. B. Eerdmans Publishing Co., 1946).

Vos, Howard F., *Beginnings in the Life of Christ* (Chicago: Moody Press, 1975).

Wuest, Kenneth S., *Mark in the Greek New Testament* (Grand Rapids: Wm. B. Eerdmans Publishing Company, 1952).

Listed below are those Bible translations specifically referred to in this study.

The Holy Bible. The Authorized Version or King James Version. Referred to in this study as KJV.

Beck, William F. *The New Testament in the Language of Today* (St. Louis: Concordia Publishing House, 1964).

New American Standard Bible (La Habra, California: The Lockman Foundation, 1960). Referred to in this study as NASB.

New International Version, New Testament (New York: New York Bible Society, 1973). Referred to in this study as NIV.

The Holy Bible. The Revised Standard Version (New York: Thomas Nelson & Sons, 1946). Referred to in this study as RSV.

Williams, Charles B., *The New Testament: A Private Translation in the Language of the People* (Chicago: Moody Press, 1949).